T0026639

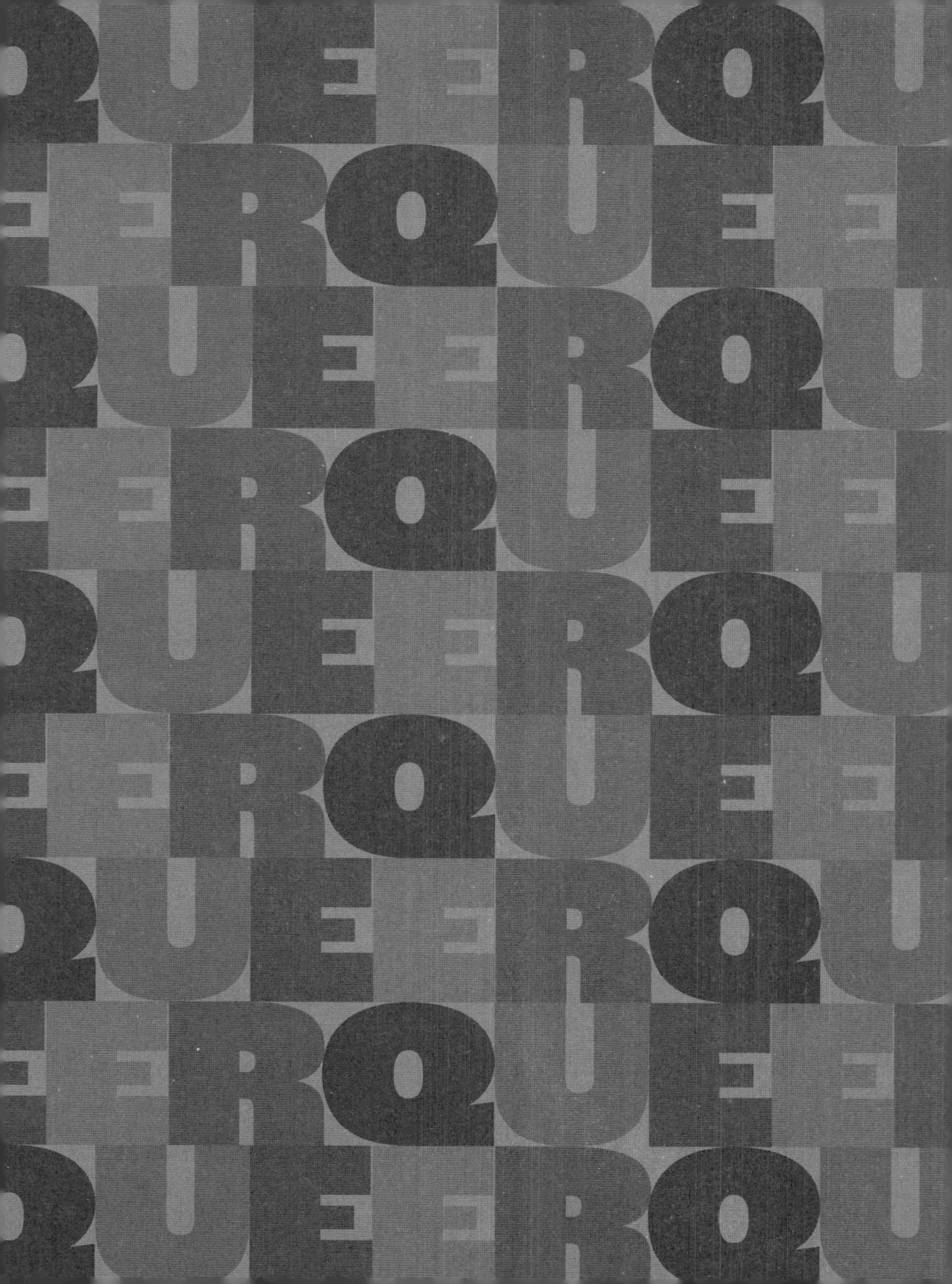

LGBTQ NATION

QUEER HERE, QUEER THERE, WE'RE NOT GOING ANYWHERE

LGBTQ+ Wit, Wisdom and Badass Affirmations

J. KATHERINE QUARTARARO

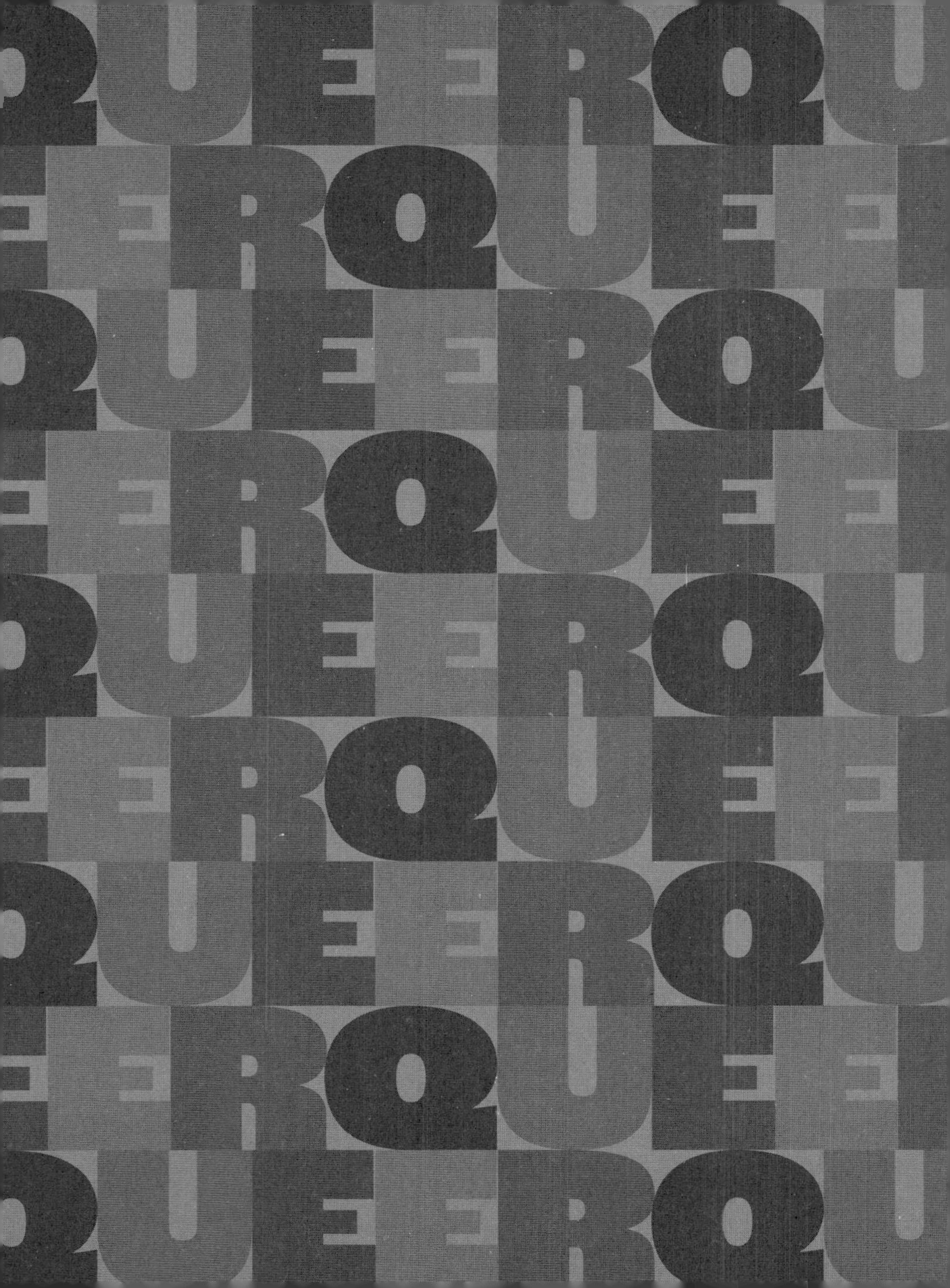

TABLE OF CONTENTS

FOREWORD

"Go kick some ass, Jim."

My bedridden husband, John, who was nearing the end of his life due to ALS, sent me out the door with those words. The reason? I was going to court. We had sued Ohio because the state would not recognize our Maryland marriage on John's last official record as an Ohio resident—his death certificate—when he died.

We sued not because we wanted a financial settlement or because we were asked to do so. We sued because we wanted to exist in the eyes of our government. We deserved and demanded that our marriage be treated no differently than any other marriage. We wanted the same rights, responsibilities and protections as any other couple.

The queer community is told at home, in school, on the street, in statehouses and in court that we are less than human and less worthy of being included in "We the People." How many queer kids will commit suicide or be murdered before that narrative ends? We are all human—more alike than different—and every person deserves affirmation of their humanity and rights. Courageous queer people throughout history risked everything to say "Enough is enough. I am here. I exist. I matter."

Thanks to them, we have made significant progress in LGBTQ+ rights, yet the pendulum always swings backward. With every step forward, people find new ways to marginalize, demonize and harm others. The queer community is not unique in this way—all marginalized communities face discrimination and hatred. But we fight on, working toward a more perfect union, one in which every person is valued, protected and respected.

Because we lack equality in society, we need support from our loved ones. Some find such love and acceptance in their families, while others find it only in their chosen family. Our family, regardless of how we define it, affirms our value and our existence.

The LGBTQ+ community is a source of belonging for millions, yet we must do better. Racism, transphobia and misogyny poison our community. We must offer and demand equality for all marginalized communities, not just our own. We have no right to ask society to affirm our rights if we are not also demanding those same rights for every other marginalized person. "We the People" means nothing unless everyone is included.

The queer community has faced erasure, hatred and discrimination, yet we refuse to be invisible, and we work to make tomorrow better than today. We must continue to fight, alongside our community and our allies, until our nation lives up to its promise of equality for all. We must work to ensure no queer kid feels alone, afraid or unloved. We will not stop until every child sees a future that includes them equally. We owe it to the courageous people who risked everything to create a better world for us, and we owe it to future generations.

Until that day, know this: We exist. We matter. We are loved.

Now go out there and kick some ass!

—Jim Obergefell

A NOTE FROM LGBTQ NATION

The privilege of covering the news that affects LGBTQ+ people is a double-edged sword. While we have the incredible opportunity to lift up queer voices and share stories of hope and resilience, we also spend our days in the trenches reporting on those who want to strip our rights away. We write about the dangerous anti-LGBTQ+ bills that have been popping up at an alarming rate across the country (including the onslaught of propaganda specifically targeting trans youth), we cover the politicians spreading hateful rhetoric about our community and we report on the violent attacks queer people endure simply for being themselves.

In these times, when it's easy to feel scared or defeated, we look to our luminaries to help lift us up, inspire us into action and remind us that we are in this fight together. It's that sense of community that makes us strong. It connects us and serves as a reminder that we're not as alone as we may have felt in school, in our hometowns or even within our own families.

Our hope is that this collection of rousing words and galvanizing anecdotes helps shine a spotlight on that connection. Some quotes will be inspiring, others will be entertaining. But as a whole, they serve as a reminder that we're not alone—we all have a voice. And together, we are making it clear we're not going anywhere.

—All of us at LGBTQ Nation
LGBTQNation.com

INTRODUCTION

When I began work on this book, I thought a lot about what I would have loved to have read when I was just coming out. Growing up in rural, conservative New England with little to no access to a queer community, I didn't know how to articulate my experience to those around me because I lacked a context in which to place those ideas. I didn't know how to be seen, because I saw no one else like me. That's merely my experience, though—this book incorporates hundreds of other voices because I alone can't speak to everyone.

Pop culture is at a point where we are seeing positive shifts toward increased representation of queer, trans and nonbinary folks, but 2022 and 2023 also saw a slew of anti-LGBTQ+ bills pass—among them the "Don't Say Gay" bill in Florida and Arkansas becoming the first state to outlaw gender-affirming health care for trans minors. That's why amplifying these voices is a vital, urgent matter.

It should also be noted that this book doesn't attempt to provide a full timeline of queer history—for that, there are many wonderful texts. Instead, it's an effort to collect the widest range of voices and stories possible. The people represented here come from different time periods and varied walks of life, which is why they offer vastly different angles on how to approach the fight for equality. What struck me in gathering these voices was the beauty and bravery contained within their lives—two virtues I aspire to channel in my everyday life. My hope is this book will be a source of inspiration to those who read it: a reminder that there is no single "right" way to be queer. This book is for that young, overwhelmed version of me as much as it is for all those who read it. Your voice, like your experience, is your own. Use it.

—J. Katherine

Visibility & Representation

Seeing ourselves in the experiences of others builds unity in the queer community as a whole.

There is strength in our numbers and diversity.... Our visibility is a sign of revolt....Remember that we are more powerful than all the hate, ignorance, and violence directed at us. Remember what a profound difference our visibility makes upon the world in which we live.

—Lani Ka'ahumanu,

one of the major architects of the American bisexual rights and visibility movement who was instrumental in organizing what would become BiNet USA, the first national bisexual rights organization. Ka'ahumanu was a founding organizer of the San Francisco Bay Area Bisexual Network (BABN) and in 1991 coedited the groundbreaking anthology Bi Any Other Name: Bisexual People Speak Out.

Gender is the poetry each of us makes out of the language we are taught.

—Leslie Feinberg,

an American radicalist, butch lesbian, transgender activist, communist and author. Her writing, notably her 1993 novel Stone Butch Blues *and her 1996 pioneering non-fiction book* Transgender Warriors, *laid the groundwork for much of the terminology and teaching of gender studies and was instrumental in bringing gender issues to a more mainstream audience.*

BEING A HOMOSEXUAL AMERICAN, I KNOW WHAT IT MEANS TO LOOK AT THE FLAG AND NOT FEEL LIKE IT PROTECTS ALL OF MY FREEDOMS.

—Megan Rapinoe,

a decorated soccer star and LGBTQ+ activist who was part of the U.S. national team that won the 2019 Women's World Cup Final.

**No one has imagined us.
We want to live like trees,/
sycamores blazing through
the sulfuric air,/ dappled with scars,
still exuberantly budding,/
our animal passion rooted in the city.**

—Adrienne Rich,
an acclaimed poet and the recipient of numerous awards and fellowships including the National Book Award, the Academy of American Poets Fellowship and a MacArthur Fellowship.

But whatever sameness I've noted in my relationships with women is not the sameness of Woman, and certainly not the sameness of parts. Rather, it is the shared, crushing understanding of what it means to live in a patriarchy.

—Maggie Nelson,
a writer whose work defies genre, spanning art criticism, personal narrative, theory and poetry as she explores topics including feminism and queerness.

I see each and every one of you. The things that make us different, those are our superpowers—every day when you walk out the door and put on your imaginary cape and go out there and conquer the world because the world would not be as beautiful as it is if we weren't in it.

—Lena Waithe,

an actor, producer and screenwriter best known for her work on the Netflix show Master of None. *Waithe was named one of* Time *magazine's 100 Most Influential People in 2018 and made* Fast Company's *Queer 50 list in 2021 and 2022.*

It takes a lot of learning to not listen to somebody else in regards to what's beautiful. Because I grew up around these rigid gender roles, when I was 18, 19, my coming-out process was about over-correcting myself in order to fit into this other part of society...Then at some point, when I was around 22, I just stopped. I was like, "I'm just going to do whatever I want and I hope that some other people follow suit."

—Theo Germaine,
a nonbinary American actor known for their role on the Netflix series The Politician.

IF I WAIT FOR SOMEONE ELSE TO VALIDATE MY EXISTENCE, IT WILL MEAN THAT I'M SHORTCHANGING MYSELF.

—Zanele Muholi,
a South African artist and activist.

MINDFUL MOMENT

I deserve to take up space.

When we don't see ourselves reflected in the world around us, it can be easy to shy away from others and dim ourselves. This simple reminder is a fundamental one; you deserve to take up space in the world. You deserve to be as bright and loud as you truly are. You are too special not to share yourself with the rest of the world.

I remember being in fifth grade. I was waiting for my bus. I remember this so weirdly and vividly, just standing by myself going, "Do I like girls?" I don't even know where it came from or why. I remember looking at this article—I think it was in *Cosmo*—that asked, "Do you want to be with that woman that you're looking at, or do you want to be her?" I was like, "I would like to be her, because she's a sexy, amazing woman, but I also want to be with her."

—LILI REINHART,
a bisexual actor known for her work on the teen drama series Riverdale.

It's just really important that we start celebrating our differences. Let's start tolerating first, but then we need to celebrate our differences.

—Billie Jean King,
an American tennis player who was formerly ranked No. 1 in the world. In addition to winning 39 Grand Slam titles, she also spearheaded the campaign for equal prize money for female tennis players at the U.S. Open and founded the Women's Tennis Association.

The next time someone asks you why LGBT Pride marches exist or why Gay Pride Month is June tell them, "A bisexual woman named Brenda Howard thought it should be."

—Brenda Howard,
a bisexual rights activist and sex-positive feminist.

MINDFUL MOMENT

I deserve to be listened to.

Being queer in a heteronormative world means your thoughts and feelings won't always align with those of others—all the more reason to share those ideas and stories. Whether you're laughing, crying, telling a story or whatever it might be, use your voice, because you deserve to be heard.

We had all of 12 or 15 people at this picnic, and that was a big turnout, a really big turnout in those days.... in the early movement it was such an unpopular thing to do. It was nonconformist at a time when most gay people were trying to blend in and pass.

—Barbara Gittings,

a poet and LGBTQ+ activist speaking about the Daughters of Bilitis (an lesbian organization founded in 1955) picnic in 1961 where she first met her life partner and fellow self-described gay rights fanatic, Kay Lahusen.

When I first started, I didn't have a trans community. I didn't know other trans people where I lived geographically, at least when I first started, so I really felt like I needed to put out a story that wasn't what I was reading. Every story I read about trans people was either sensationalist, or someone was dead.

—Thomas Page McBee,

speaking on his memoir Man Alive, *which was published in 2014. In 2018, he went on to publish a second memoir,* Amateur: A True Story About What Makes a Man, *in which he chronicles his experiences becoming the first trans man to box at Madison Square Garden.*

LGBT people are some of the bravest and most potent change agents and leaders I have encountered, and the most forceful defenders of the vulnerable and voiceless, because they know what it's like to be there.

—Ronan Farrow,

a journalist known for his investigative work for The New Yorker *detailing the sexual allegations against Harvey Weinstein, which won the Pulitzer Prize in 2018. That year, Farrow publicly identified as part of the LGBTQ+ community.*

There will not be a magic day when we wake up and it's now okay to express ourselves publicly. We make that day by doing things publicly until it's simply the way things are.

–Tammy Baldwin,

a Wisconsin Senator and the first openly gay woman elected to the House of Representatives (1999) and Senate (2013).

I AM PROUD THAT I FOUND THE COURAGE TO DEAL THE INITIAL BLOW TO THE HYDRA OF PUBLIC CONTEMPT.

—Karl Heinrich Ulrichs,

one of the first gay men to publicly announce his sexual identity. Born in Germany in 1825, his coming out was a historic and brave moment. He first wrote about his sexuality through a series of essays under a pseudonym, and after his books were banned throughout Germany, he came out publicly in front of the Congress of German Jurists in Munich to urge a repeal of anti-homosexual laws. During his lifetime, Ulrichs wrote numerous essays discussing homosexuality and asserting that non-heterosexual orientations are natural and biological.

During this pandemic, and over a year spent largely isolated, many queer people could not go to safe spaces or be in community, and for many of us, queer media was a refuge. For people living in unsupportive areas or who might be closeted, queer media has been, and continues to be, a lifeline. Today, it feels like there is more queer content than ever, but as more companies begin to see our community as profitable, curiously they are also less likely to believe that they need those of us with lived experience to create content for us. ....There may be more films featuring queer people, but it is still far too rare to see films that feature LGBTQ+ actors, writers, or directors. For so long, stories about our community were considered niche; more accurately, they were considered controversial and incendiary.

—Andrea L. Pino-Silva,
an activist, author and public scholar.

I've never met a gay person who regretted coming out—including myself. Life at last begins to make sense, when you are open and honest.

—Sir Ian McKellen,
a British actor known for his roles in the Lord of the Rings *and* X-Men *franchises.*

I've always kind of put myself in the ally category because I had some weird narrative about not deserving to be a part of the LGBTQ community. I don't know what that is. Some inborn self-judgment [or] self-imposed something. But...I'm a member part of this, I'm not just an ally....It feels very vulnerable. It feels very exposed and different, but I'm surfing this new wave and it's been really special.

—Dove Cameron,
an American singer and actress who got her start on the Disney Channel. In 2018, she won a Daytime Emmy for Outstanding Performer in a Children's Program for Liv and Maddie.

In my private life, it's been going on for a long time. I obviously don't really identify as a straight woman ever in my life, but I feel like now I'm really in my queerness. I'm in L.A. living my *L Word* life. Isn't it amazing?

—Barbie Ferreira,
a Brazilian-American model and actor who appeared on two seasons of HBO's Euphoria.

MINDFUL MOMENT

I'm glad I'm here and so are others.

The world had to do a lot of conspiring in order for you to end up in this very spot, at this very moment, which is all to say you are here for a reason. Remember to be glad for that and remember how much joy you bring to those around you. They don't want you to be anyone but yourself, and neither should you.

The most important thing about [the bookstore] is, it was going to be an openly gay, visible presence on the street. I've always firmly believed, and I think today it's just as important as ever, that we always be visible in every possible circumstance. To me, it's always been the nitty-gritty of the movement, what the movement really is all about. Not only as an example to younger gay people, but as a poke in the ribs to society in general.

—Craig Rodwell,
an activist who opened the world's first gay bookstore, the Oscar Wilde Memorial Bookshop, in NYC in 1967.

If you're gay and you can't hold hands, or you're Black and you can't catch a taxi, or you're a woman and you can't go into the park, you are aware there's a menace. That's costly on a psychic level. The world should be striving to make all its members secure.

—Tony Kushner,

a Tony award-winning author and playwright whose groundbreaking work Angels in America, *an examination of AIDS and homosexuality in America in the 1980s, won the Pulitzer Prize.*

I've always felt the way I've felt. It wasn't a new feeling; it was just the discovery of a language and a community of people that felt the same way. It's been lovely. It's been a process of feeling heard and seen—that there is a space that I can live in and enjoy my life in and feel completely like myself, and be treated as such.

—Sam Smith,

a British pop star who came out as nonbinary in 2019—one of the first major celebrities to do so. Smith, and trans singer Kim Petras, are the first nonbinary and trans artists to top the Billboard Top 100 with their song "Unholy."

When I got to the script for *Billions* and the character breakdown for Taylor Mason, the character that I play, said female and nonbinary, a little light bulb went off in my head…I did a little bit of research and discovered that female is an assigned sex and nonbinary is in reference to gender identity and those are two different things. It finally helped me put language to a feeling that I'd had my entire life.

—Asia Kate Dillon,

an American actor known for their roles on Orange is the New Black *and* Billions. *Their character on* Billions *was the first nonbinary main character to appear on North American television. Dillon has been nominated for three Critics Choice Awards.*

One of the greatest things L.A. has given me is awareness. I realized there's a spectrum and different ways people identify. I started meeting different people and went, "Am I attracted to women? I've always felt close to friends who were girls, but is this a thing?" I only allowed myself to experiment and discover once I realized the possibilities.

—Lilly Singh,

a Canadian actress, comedian and talk show host who rose to fame with her YouTube channel, which boasted nearly 15 million subscribers at its height.

I want to be visible to queer folks who don't see people like them on their feed. I know it saved my life years ago. I want to challenge cis folks (if you don't know what cis means, that's probably you!!!) to be better allies.

—QUINN,
a Canadian soccer player and Olympic gold medalist.

MINDFUL MOMENT

My queerness has enabled me to explore and get to know myself better than I ever have.

When you can embrace your queerness as a beautiful strength, the ways in which it can empower you become much more clear. Your queerness gives depth to your thoughts and experiences; it becomes this lens filtering the world in a way only other queer folk can relate to—pretty special, huh? Repeat this affirmation daily to remind yourself of the wonder of queerness.

WHEN I WAS IN THE MILITARY, THEY GAVE ME A MEDAL FOR KILLING TWO MEN AND A DISCHARGE FOR LOVING ONE.

—LEONARD MATLOVICH,
who served in the Air Force during the Vietnam War and fought the military's ban on gays. He became a household name and face (even ending up on the cover of Time *magazine) for gay rights in the 1970s.*

All the girls would go to the Promenade to hang out with cute boys, and it made me feel very alone. It was depressing to watch girls that I liked flirt with guys. So I just stayed home.... My first [female-identifying] friend who liked girls really changed my life because she was comfortable with who she was. It made me want to be comfortable with who I was.

—HAYLEY KIYOKO,
an American actress, dancer, singer and LGBTQ+ activist.

At that time it was considered a criminal act. In fact, I remember being picked up by the front of my shirt and slapped back and forth by a policeman because I was on the streets at 11 o'clock [at night] and I had on slacks, women's slacks[,] and a sports shirt.... I wasn't frightened, I was angry. He had no right to do that to me. And that's been my attitude all of my life. They have no right.

—Shirley Willer,
on her first time going to a gay bar. Willer eventually went on to become the national president of the Daughters of Bilitis, the first lesbian organization in the U.S.

Seeing people from all over the world come to New York to celebrate Pride was really inspiring. What I love is that it brings people together to celebrate not only what we have in common but how we are different.

—Alexander Wang,
an American fashion designer.

Just as gay people have to become visible in the society, lesbians had to become visible, because whenever people said gay, they always thought about gay men. We sat around, actually, for months and tried to figure out what were the women's issues that were different from feminist issues, or different from gay issues. And quite frankly, to this day, no one has been able to come up with what those issues are. But it's a matter of attitude. It's a matter of positioning. It's a matter of respect. It's a matter of power. It's a matter of all those types of things, which are a little more subtle.... and visibility, of course, visibility. Just having people realize that there are lesbians in the world and when you say "gay" it has to include gay men and women.

—JEAN O'LEARY,
a vocal activist whose comments at a Gay Pride Gala rally in 1973 disparaging men who dressed as women caused a lot of scrutiny. She later expressed regret for having taken such a strong stance against trans women in an interview with gay historian Eric Marcus in 1989.

That's why when I watched Joe and Frankie [who play a gay couple in *High School Musical: The Musical: The Series*] film the scene in Season 1, Episode 5, "Homecoming," where for the first time they danced together, I just remember full body chills, weeping. I didn't connect the dots why until recently... the reason that made me so emotional. I'm getting so emotional now because they were speaking their truth despite the inevitable reaction that they were going to get.

—JOSHUA BASSETT,
an American actor, singer and songwriter known for his starring role on High School Musical: The Musical: The Series.

THE SINGLE BEST THING ABOUT COMING OUT OF THE CLOSET IS THAT NOBODY CAN INSULT YOU BY TELLING YOU WHAT YOU'VE JUST TOLD THEM.

—RACHEL MADDOW,
an American television news host and political commentator. Maddow came out publicly as a 17-year-old student at Stanford, where she was interviewed, alongside the only other out lesbian on campus, by the student newspaper. She is the first openly lesbian anchor to host a primetime news program in the U.S.

MINDFUL MOMENT

My experience matters.

Do you wake up every morning fully believing that your experience as a human on this vast planet matters? As much as any other creature? Well, it does. It's an easy thing to forget, but it makes a major difference. The ups, the downs, the trials and tribulations, the joys and celebrations—it all matters.

Gays and lesbians have been stereotyped by society. By sharing our experiences—both good and bad, enriching and unhappy—we humanize who we are. The lives and experiences of all of us are different and specific to each individual and by sharing those experiences, we cease to be seen as the cartoons that were imposed on us.

—George Takei,

an American actor, writer and activist known for his role on the original Star Trek *series. Takei had an asteroid named after him in 2007.*

I can't remember who described [pansexuality] to me, but it was basically like, "That's who you are when you love anyone and everyone." I was like, "Great. That's what I am." It just stuck, and I ran with it... I thought I was straight my whole life because nobody presented any other option. I didn't know any queer people. Nobody in my family is queer. The older I got, the more access I had to the internet and I got to see other people living lives that were nothing like the one I had in front of me.

—MADISON BAILEY,
an American actor known for her work on the Netflix teen drama Outer Banks.

I really, honestly think that anybody who is openly gay and visible is powerful. It doesn't matter what you do, you are impacting people.

—PORTIA DE ROSSI,
an American actor best known for her work on the series Arrested Development *who has been married to Ellen DeGeneres since 2008.*

I'm a young, bisexual woman, and I've spent a large part of my life trying to validate myself—to my friends, to my family, to myself—trying to prove that who I love and the way that I feel is not a phase. It's not part of some confusion that's going to change or could be manipulated.

—Halsey,
an American singer who has long used her public platform to speak out about issues for the LGBQT+ community—including homelessness rates for LGBQT+ youth. She also uses her social media to share intimate details with fans, including when she updated her pronouns to "she/they" via Instagram in March 2021.

The Stonewall riots were a key moment for gay people. Throughout modern history, gays had thought of themselves as something like a mental illness or maybe a sin or a crime. Gay liberation allowed us to make the leap to being a "minority group," which made life much easier.

—Edmund White,
an American novelist, memoirist, playwright and biographer.

I want to make sure that any young person or anyone really who is looking up to me—who sees a glimpse of who I am as a person—that they see no shame, that they see pride, and that I'm truly unabashed about the person that I am.

—Samira Wiley,
an American actor who starred as Poussey on the Netflix series Orange Is the New Black.

MINDFUL MOMENT

My words are powerful.

Your words are an extension of yourself—don't forget about this power. And don't be overwhelmed by it, either. Just remind yourself through the use of this affirmation that the words you choose to speak and write have weight; they have the potential to speak to a deeper truth. Who knew wielding a superpower could be so easy?

I don't want to seem presumptuous, because everyone has their own experience. The whole issue of sexuality is so gray. I'm just trying to acknowledge that fluidity, that grayness, which has always existed. But maybe only now are we allowed to start talking about it.

—Kristen Stewart,
an American actor known for her roles in the Twilight *saga as well as the films* Certain Women *(2016) and* Personal Shopper *(2016).*

I have built a career out of self-deprecating humor and I don't want to do that anymore. Do you understand what self-deprecation means when it comes from somebody who already exists in the margins? It's not humility, it's humiliation. I put myself down in order to speak, in order to seek permission to speak, and I simply will not do that anymore, not to myself or anybody who identifies with me. If that means that my comedy career is over, then so be it.

—Hannah Gadsby,
an Australian comedian known for her acclaimed Netflix special Nanette. *Rather than ruin her career, the candid special brought Gadsby an unexpected level of fame.*

Whether the unsympathetic majority approves or not, it looks as though the third sex is here to stay. With the advancement of psychiatry and related subjects, the world is becoming more and more aware that there are those in our midst who feel no attraction for the opposite sex. It is not an uncommon sight to observe mannishly attired women or even those dressed in more feminine garb strolling along the street hand-in-hand or even arm-in-arm, in an attitude which certainly would seem to indicate far more than mere friendliness.

—Edythe Eyde,

from the September 1947 issue of her magazine, Vice Versa. *The magazine, which was subtitled "America's Gayest Magazine," is the earliest known U.S. lesbian publication. Though the magazine only ran from 1947 to 1948, it set the agenda that defined lesbian and gay journalism in the decades that followed.*

I could not in good faith move forward with denying any part of my identity to conform to a system and structure that does not hold space for people like me.

—Justin David Sullivan,

a nonbinary actor who withdrew from consideration for the Tony Awards, citing the lack of non-gendered categories. Sullivan plays the nonbinary character May in the Shakespearean jukebox musical & Juliet.

You are the ultimate power and you have never been so visible in the world! And that beautiful light and that rainbow is shining all around you. Stand in it. Bask in it. Allow yourself to glow in it as we grow. Take that spotlight, it belongs to you.

—Lady Gaga,

an American pop star and actor known for her avant-garde style. Her deep support of the LGBTQ+ community over the years has included wearing a meat dress as a form of protest against the military's "Don't Ask, Don't Tell" policy; her 2011 single "Born This Way," which instantly became a gay anthem; and when she helped get the word out to vote the year gay marriage was on the ballot in the U.S.

It's the principle. I didn't ask to be put in this position, but I'm here. And along with being honest, the other thing my mother taught me somehow along the way is do the best you can. That's all we can ask of you. That's all. And so I do.

—Perry Watkins,
an American soldier and one of the first people to challenge the military's ban on homosexuals.

It's about everyone being able to feel acknowledged and represented. It's difficult for me at the moment trying to justify in my head being nonbinary and being nominated in female categories. When it comes to categories, do we need to make it specific as to whether you're being nominated for a female role or a male role?

—Emma Corrin,
a British actor who starred as Princess Diana in the Netflix show The Crown.

Whenever the occasion came up for gay people to speak on gay issues, I would always volunteer. Whether that meant on radio talk shows, on panels, colleges, the media, newspapers, anything and everything. And I think it was becoming more open about my gayness. I was also being a lot more politically involved because of the need to come out even more.

—Zandra Rolón,

a gay rights activist. Rolón and her partner were refused service at a restaurant in L.A. in 1983 after which they filed a civil lawsuit against the restaurant. The couple eventually won their case, which went all the way to the Supreme Court, and it set the precedent for other cases of LGBTQ+ discrimination.

The things that we were working on in the '50s in the Daughters of Bilitis was trying to build our self esteem—to say that we were okay in spite of being faced with...being [called] immoral, illegal, and sick. I mean that's heavy duty for a lot of people.

—Del Martin,

a lesbian rights activist.

MINDFUL MOMENT

I am enough and I have always been enough.

It's important to remember that there's nothing we need to do to prove our worth to either ourselves or anyone else—we are beautiful, imperfect, fully whole beings. You are enough, you have always been enough and you will always be enough.

**In 1956, at the age of 5,
I prayed for God to turn me into a girl.
The word "transgender" wouldn't be created
and popularized for another 20 years.
I couldn't even read or write,
but I knew I had been born in the wrong body.
I hid my identity for over four decades,
but at the age of 48, I finally began living
the truth I knew at 5 years old.**

—Monica Helms,
cofounder of the Transgender American Veterans Association and creator of the original Trans Pride flag.

I really *was* a sissy.... I walked differently than the boys did, and I knew that I felt differently than the boys did. I knew I saw differently than the boys did, and I had a tendency to cry. And I liked poetry and all those things that boys are not supposed to like. And they would call me a fairy and I knew that fairy was a terrible word, but I kinda liked it. Secretly, I liked it.

—Harry Hay,
an American gay rights activist and labor advocate.

I knew I was gay from the day I was born. And I think there have been—I now know that there were experiences all through, before I even got to Yale, and they were all covert and guilt-inducing on everybody's part. So it seemed as if all those early years were spent trying to deny these feelings.

—Larry Kramer,
an American author, playwright, producer and gay rights activist.

MINDFUL MOMENT

I live an authentic life.

No one aside from you knows what "authentic" means in the context of your life. But you feel it, you know deep down when things are bringing you closer to your truest self or when they're pulling you further away. As you pay attention to the vibrations of your experiences throughout the day, try to identify exactly what authenticity means for you. It'll be different from everyone else's personal definition, but tell yourself you will honor your authenticity every day.

I was sitting with some friends having a sandwich or something at Mama's Chicken Rib, a popular gay coffee shop on Greenwich Avenue. And this demonstration went by. Hundreds of people with protest signs and chanting and...obviously a gay demonstration. And I said to my friends at the table, "Let's join it." Nobody wanted to join it. I said, "Well, I'll see you later." I wasn't going to let the parade go by.

—Morty Manford,

on his transition from observer to activist. In addition to his activist work with the gay community, Manford also served as an Assistant New York State attorney general.

They used to take us to the movies every Saturday, and I was crazy only about the women. It was the only thing that I would focus on. You know what it is? You recognize difference before you recognize sameness. And I didn't feel the same as everybody else.

—Joyce Hunter,

an LGBTQ+ activist who cofounded the Harvey Milk High School, an alternative high school for at-risk LGBTQ+ youth in NYC.

There were 27 reasons why you could lose your teacher's license in California at this time, above all if you were a card carrying Communist or a suspected homosexual.

—Billye Talmadge,

an early member of the Daughters of Bilitis, the first organization for lesbians in the United States, which was founded in 1955.

My advice as lesbian/queer elder and *Curve* politics editor is: Tell your stories, tell our stories, never ever let someone else take your voice and tell that story in their words and their revision. There is not yet a place for us at the table of power.

—Victoria A. Brownworth,
an American journalist, writer and editor.

Even though when I watched [*Will & Grace*] I didn't feel like I'm Jack or I'm Will. I didn't feel like that was me on screen. But just that there was a show where people were gay and they were interacting with each other, I breathed a little sigh of relief. You don't feel as alone, like you're the only person.

—Jonathan Groff,
an American actor and singer who appeared in the original Broadway casts of Spring Awakening *and* Hamilton. *He's also appeared on* Glee *as well as the Netflix show* Mindhunter.

I think lesbian visibility is one of those reasons that I became a writer. You know, I wanted to feel like I'm not like some ghost or shadow or some hypothetical, you know. I'm a real person, a real woman who's had effects on the culture and on the politics and been at the core of much of the activism in the 20th century. And you should be able to see who I am and who we are. So, I'm going to go outside my house for Lesbian Visibility Day.

—JEWELLE GOMEZ,
an American author, poet, critic and playwright.

I was fine being in the closet at the beginning of my career because that's what you were supposed to be—until I realized that it didn't serve anybody, and I was left feeling utterly empty. This is who I am, so I've gotta be me.

—BILLY PORTER,
an Emmy Award-winning actor known for his role in Pose *as well as for his fearless gender nonconforming red carpet fashion.*

My earliest memories of queerness come from pop culture.... I remember we'd watch MTV, which was brand new, and that's where I saw Boy George. I was so enamored of him. It didn't not make sense to me. I never thought: So that's a boy dressed as a girl? Wearing makeup? It was almost like it was home.

—Beth Ditto,

an American singer, songwriter and actor who is best known for her indie rock band, Gossip, which was active from 1999 to 2016.

Yes, we have more GLBT characters. My issues are: What are those characters doing on those shows? Are they just saying so-and-so is gay, and then we don't actually deal with the fact that they're gay? We don't actually see them have a partner or even see their lives.

—Wilson Cruz,
an actor famous for being the first openly gay actor to play an openly gay TV character: Ricky on My So-Called Life *(1994–1995).*

MINDFUL MOMENT

I remain true to myself in all that I say and do.

Whether it's because we don't want to offend others or because we don't feel secure enough to share our thoughts, there are many reasons why we as queer people might bend to the world around us. And we know how terrible that type of contortion feels. Remember that who you are at your core (your queerness) is beautiful. Knowing this makes it much easier to remain true to yourself in all that you say and do in your daily life.

A light bulb went off. The word didn't make me feel marginalized. It made me feel less crazy. It made me feel less alone. It gave me hope... Because of the voices I listened to, because of the people I identified with, the films I had watched, the music I had heard—because of words like "bisexual" and the doors that it opened—I'm still here.

—Evan Rachel Wood,
an actress who received the Human Rights Campaign's LGBTQ Visibility Award.

Without a visual identity, we have no community, no support network, no movement. Making ourselves visible is a political act, making ourselves visible is a continual process.

—Joan E. Biren,
an American photographer and filmmaker who focuses on the lives of LGBTQ+ people.

I have been a lesbian all my life, for eighty-two years, and I am proud of myself and my people. I would like all my people to be free in this world, my gay people and my Black people.

—Mabel Hampton,
an American lesbian activist and dancer during the Harlem Renaissance.

The next generation is so far advanced over us. I love that a lot of younger people now come out that would never have come out in the old days. Of course, they are born into a community already. They just have to discover it, whereas we were still building it.

—Edith Windsor,
an activist whose 2013 case against the Defense of Marriage Act led the Supreme Court to grant same-sex couples federal rights for the very first time.

THE POWER OF VISIBILITY CAN NEVER BE UNDERESTIMATED.

—Margaret Cho,
comedian and actor.

Let me be to someone else what no one was to me. Let me send a message to that kid, maybe in America, maybe someplace far overseas, maybe somewhere deep inside—a kid who is being targeted at home or at school or in the streets—that someone is watching and listening and caring, that there is an "us," that there is a "we," and that kid or teenager or adult is loved and they are not alone.

—Wentworth Miller,
an actor best known for his work on the TV series Prison Break.

MINDFUL MOMENT

I speak with confidence.

Speaking with confidence is achieved by remembering that we don't need others to validate our thoughts or ideas in order for them to have worth. As we've already touched on in this chapter, we as queer people have an innate worth and value—and therefore our ideas do, too. With this in mind, speak proudly and share that confidence with the rest of the world.

I don't mean to sound trite when I say this, but the single most important thing that we can do as LGBT people is to come out.

—Brian Sims,
a politician who first worked as the president of Equality Pennsylvania and was also the chairman of the Gay and Lesbian Lawyers of Philadelphia (GALLOP). When he was voted into the state House of Representatives in 2012, he became the first openly gay person elected to the Pennsylvania General Assembly.

What I liked about the rainbow is that it fits all of us. It's all the colors. It represents all the genders. It represents all the races. It's the rainbow of humanity.

—Gilbert Baker,
an artist, designer, activist and creator of the rainbow pride flag.

Amazing how eye and skin color come in many shades yet many think sexuality is just gay or straight.

—DaShanne Stokes,
an author, sociologist and public speaker.

One promise that I made to myself is that when my rugby career ended, I would continue to live the rest of my life in the identity, in the body that I should have.... All you have to do is turn on the TV, look on social media platforms, and you see the amount of bullying, harm, and discrimination that goes on about gender identities.... So for someone to be open and honest about that in the public eye is absolutely daunting.

—Ellia Green,
an Australian rugby player who is the first Olympic athlete to come out as a trans man.

My intervention is evolution—I'm just another person transitioning. I'm showing gender fluidity; how fast and dynamic and vulnerable it can be, how it's an ongoing thing.

—Tommy Dorfman,

an American actress best known for her role on Netflix's 13 Reasons Why. *She was later honored with the Rising Star Award by GLAAD in 2017.*

MINDFUL MOMENT

I express myself clearly and openly.

Imagine how freeing it might feel to say exactly what you mean, regardless of the context, the situation or the audience. You can feel that freedom every day if you remind yourself of this affirmation. Again, believing that the things you're expressing have worth and value can make it easier to convey them clearly and openly.

[In] 1949 [in L.A.] there were restaurants you could go to, there were hotels that a mixed couple could stay in—not many, but some. This was the most wide open city in America in the '40s, a rip-roaring town. There was open male-to-male dancing to live music in gay bars in the city, and I've done it. And that was not happening in any other city in America to our knowledge. So that what we were able to, what the movement was able to do, was to slip through the cracks and become strong enough to survive.

—Dorr Legg,
an American architect and leader of the gay rights movement in the 1950s.

If you got caught, you got thrown out of the Navy. That much I knew. And there were people thrown off the ship while I was there for being gay, who had been caught in the act on the ship, which is almost always what happens.

—Vernon E. "Copy" Berg III,
who served in the Navy, was discharged in 1976 and then challenged the military's longstanding ban on homosexuals. He went on to become an activist, alongside his partner, E. Lawrence Gibson, for gay rights.

Creating a strong, black, other, queer male is something that really needed to happen because you don't see that that often, especially not in hip-hop.

—Ojay Morgan,
a rapper who goes by the name Zebra Katz.

It took me years to overcome my own internalized homophobia and find my community. The most encouraging thing to help me was *seeing other people like me*. Growing up there was only one person throughout all my years of school who reflected me, and she was my butch lesbian PE teacher. Unfortunately, she was also the butt of everyone's joke and an outsider. So instead of being a beacon, she felt more like a warning for me to stay in the closet.... So, as a fully self-aware and beautiful butch lesbian, I'm here to tell you the importance of being out, proud and *visible*!

—Shaley Howard,
a writer and organizer.

MINDFUL MOMENT

I am connected to my truth.

Our truth is the core of our being, so staying connected to that deeper sense of self can act as an anchor throughout our day. Whether we speak it, draw it, write it or simply just feel it, use each day as an opportunity to stay connected with your truth, and allow it to be a healing, grounding force throughout your day.

Love & Fulfillment

Before we can truly give ourselves to others, we must embrace ourselves wholeheartedly.

When I was like, "I am fully interested in pursuing this relationship," it did feel like I was saying yes to spending my life with someone, because I was so in love. And I think that's, for me personally, what it took to understand my sexuality. Some people, for whatever reason, get there sooner.

—STEPHANIE ALLYNNE,
an actor known for films such as In A World, *on her relationship with comedian Tig Notaro.*

When I refuse to make myself smaller to accommodate the demands for respectability put forward by mainstream institutions—when I wear sheer dresses and chokers to art openings and airports alike, when I don't tuck, when I am my fullest and freest self in the most public of places—I'm freedom dreaming. I am expanding in the power of my unruliness and refusal to conform to violent and oppressive normativity.

—Tourmaline,
a trans activist and filmmaker. She codirected the short film Happy Birthday, Marsha! *(2017) about legendary activist Marsha P. Johnson and directed the short film* Salacia *(2019) about a trans woman in New York in the 1800s who was outed.*

OPENNESS MAY NOT COMPLETELY DISARM PREJUDICE, BUT IT'S A GOOD PLACE TO START.

—Jason Collins,
a former professional basketball player and only the second openly gay athlete to play in a professional sports league in the U.S. or Canada.

MINDFUL MOMENT

I deserve love without conditions.

The relationships we have—whether they're romantic, platonic or everything in between—all deserve the fullest versions of us. If someone else makes us feel as though we have to hide any part of ourselves, that relationship is toxic and it's time to get out. Anyone who truly loves us would never want us to be anything but ourselves.

Like all marginalized people in our white supremacist patriarchal nation, every day that we choose to love ourselves and each other is a radical act of war against the people who would rather see us dead than happy. They are so threatened by our joy that they routinely kill us while we dance. They kill us while we celebrate life. They know that our self-love, our sense of community, undermines the entire system they've constructed.

—E.R. Fightmaster,

an American actor who plays Kai Bartley on Grey's Anatomy, *the first nonbinary doctor ever featured in the long-running network TV series.*

The fact is, I'm gay, always have been, always will be, and I couldn't be any more happy, comfortable with myself and proud.... Visibility is important, more important than preserving my reporter's shield.

—ANDERSON COOPER,

a broadcast journalist and political commentator who publicly came out in 2012, nine years after his CNN show Anderson Cooper 360° *began. His work has earned him 12 Emmy awards and two Peabody Awards.*

The more I hold myself close
and fully embrace who I am,
the more I dream,
the more my heart grows
and the more I thrive.

—Elliot Page,
a Canadian actor, producer, director and LGBTQ+ activist who publicly came out as transgender in December 2020. He's been nominated for an Academy Award, three BAFTA Awards, two Emmy Awards and is the first openly trans man to appear on the cover of Time.

**I want you to know your gayness or your transness, your gender nonconformity, your intersex status are all beautiful.
I want you to know that if you are LGBTQI+ and a person of color, [or] have a disability you are beautiful.
If you don't feel the love in your immediate surroundings it's out there for you.
I believe that by being a beacon of love, you can eventually draw that love to you.
Don't give up hope.**

—Laverne Cox,
an actor and outspoken trailblazer for the trans community. Cox is perhaps best known for her role as Sophia on Orange is the New Black, *for which she became the first transgender woman to be nominated for an Emmy.*

The continual process of unlearning heteronormativity and internalized homophobia can be difficult, but one of the biggest blessings lies in the magic that comes from having to understand love outside the confines of learned heterosexual roles.

—Amandla Stenberg,
an American actor who made Time's *list of Most Influential Teens in both 2015 and 2016. Some of her other accolades include a Teen Choice Award, an NAACP Image Award and nominations for three Black Reel Awards and a Critics Choice Award.*

After a long internal journey, you now embrace being gay, recognizing it as a wonderful and integrally important component part of the totality that is you.

—Neil Patrick Harris,
an American actor who rose to fame for his starring role in the late 1980s series Doogie Howser, M.D. *Over the course of his career, he has earned four Emmy awards, a Tony award and a Grammy nomination.*

I want people to fall in love with themselves and to be really proud and full of joy for the space they take up. If someone else appreciates the space you take up, then that's icing on the cake.

—Jonathan Van Ness,

a writer, TV personality, hairstylist, podcast host and overall pop culture icon who rose to fame as a member of the Fab Five on the Queer Eye *reboot in 2018. Van Ness is an outspoken activist for the LGBTQ+ community and identifies as nonbinary.*

I feel normal at last.
Everyone has been so accepting...
I haven't lost anything—my career,
my fans, my friends—but I've gained so much.
I came home from that game
and went straight to my mum and dad's.
They cracked open a bottle of champagne.
I didn't know what we were toasting
but my mother was like:
"The rest of your life."

—Gareth Thomas,
a former professional Welsh rugby player—a sport for which he was the most capped (a designation for making the most appearances on the field for his country) until 2011. After coming out in 2009, Thomas was voted the most influential gay person of 2010 on The Independent on Sunday *Pink List (now called the Rainbow List).*

I've never considered my relationship with [my husband] Todd to be an act of activism. Rather, it is simply an act of love—coffee in the morning, going to work, washing the clothes, taking the dogs [out]—a regular life, boring love.

—Jim Parsons,
an American actor best known for his work on The Big Bang Theory.

MINDFUL MOMENT

I will give myself love without conditions.

All that we should come to expect from the people we have relationships with also applies to the relationship we have with ourselves. That unconditional love is something we can give to ourselves every day—perfection isn't the point, and perfection isn't the only thing worthy of love. The more we can find to love about our messy, imperfect selves, the better.

In loving him, I saw a cigarette between the fingers of a hand, smoke blowing backwards into the room and sputtering planes diving low through the clouds. In loving him, I saw men encouraging each other to lay down their arms. In loving him, I saw small-town laborers creating excavations that other men spend their lives trying to fill.

—David Wojnarowicz,

an American artist who was a prominent fixture in the East Village art scene, who used numerous forms of media to draw attention to civil rights and gay rights throughout the 1980s.

YOU DON'T FALL IN LOVE WITH THE GENDER; YOU FALL IN LOVE WITH THE PERSON.

—Sandra Alva,

an American musician who currently plays drums in the post-hardcore band, Modern Day Escape. She previously played in the band Black Veil Brides.

Too late, too late, your love gave me life. Here am I the creature you made through your loving; by your passion you created the thing that I am. Who are you to deny me the right to love? But for you I need never have known existence.

—Radclyffe Hall,

from her novel The Well of Loneliness *(1928), a groundbreaking work in lesbian literature. The book was banned shortly after its publication. As an adult, Hall often went by the name John, rather than her birth name, Marguerite.*

MINDFUL MOMENT

It is a joy and a privilege to get to know the true me.

When the world around us doesn't always seem to like or respect us, it can be hard to embrace ourselves completely. But it's vital—and meeting ourselves with an attitude of acceptance sets the tone for others to meet us with openness and acceptance as well. Getting to know yourself should be an incredible joy.

You only live once, so never be afraid to be you.... The LGBTQ+ community is amazing and we all love you and support you. We know it's scary, but trust me, you are so loved. We are all here to be there with you through your journey.

—DANIELLE COHN,

founder of the first teen-owned feminine care brand, Feel Divine. The brand's plant-based products are designed to help tweens and teens develop self-awareness and self-confidence. With over 19 million followers on TikTok, Cohn was also voted one of GLAAD's 20 under 20 Outstanding Young LGBTQ Changemakers in 2022.

Being a lesbian means I have the opportunity to love what is uncommon, and I'm okay with that. I do not cry myself to sleep or [get] upset by the life that I lead because of who I care about. Because I accept the fact that it is simply love.

—JENNA EMBERS,

a YouTube star who gained a strong following with her channel Lesbian Answers, where she discussed a variety of LGBTQ+-related issues.

For me, sexuality and sexual identity and fluidity *is* a journey. It's not a destination. I've discovered so much about myself over the years as I've evolved and grown and spent time with myself and loved ones. That's the exciting thing— always finding out new things about who you are. And that's what I love about life. It takes us on journeys that not even we ourselves sometimes are prepared for. You just adapt to where you are and how you've evolved as a free thinking person.

—Janelle Monáe,
an American singer, rapper and actor. Her many accolades include eight Grammy nominations, an MTV Video Music Award, an ASCAP Vanguard Award and a Billboard Women in Music Rising Star Award.

Dance until your bones clatter. What a prize/ you are. What a lucky sack of stars.

—Gabrielle Calvocoressi,

from her poetry collection, Apocalyptic Swing *(2009).*
The American poet has been the recipient of numerous awards and fellowships including the Audre Lorde Award for Lesbian Poetry.

Crushes are very strange things; they're a warning sign in the word itself—crush: to deform, pulverize, or force inward by compressing forcefully. Whoever decided it was a good idea to equate deformity and compression to blooming affection was either very high or a genius—or maybe lost somewhere in between. But for good or bad, I could feel it: my heart pressing inward until the sound of it beating filled my ears again.

—A. N. Casey,

from his queer YA novel, Permanent Jet Lag *(2017).*
The book was honored in the Rainbow Awards, an annual contest celebrating outstanding work in LGBTQ+ fiction and nonfiction.

In fact, we, the LGBTQ+ community, have always been here. We were required to lead invisible lives out of necessity. We loved who we loved in the background of society because it was too dangerous to do otherwise.

—Gayla Turner,

from her nonfiction book, Don't You Dare: Uncovering Lost Love *(2022). The book chronicles Turner's discovery of her grandmother's secret marriage to a woman in the early 1900s as well as a hidden lesbian social club in a small town in Wisconsin.*

WHAT I KNOW MOST ABOUT THEIR HATE IS THAT IT CAN'T BEAT THE LOVE OUT OF ME.

—Andrea Gibson,

an American poet and activist whose work focuses on gender norms, politics, social reform and LGBTQ+ topics.

My heart knows who I am and who I'll turn out to be!

—E. Lynn Harris,

from his novel Invisible Life *(1991). Openly gay, he's known for books featuring closeted African-American male characters.*

I hope you learn to love yourself for who you are and what you look like, and how you were born to be, because you are perfect in your own way.

—Tyler Oakley,

an American influencer, actor, activist and author. Much of Oakley's activism has been dedicated to health care, education and suicide prevention among LGBTQ+ youth. He primarily uses Instagram to reach his 6 million followers.

The weight of him pressed me out.
I felt covered, safe; something dark in me
retreated and, for what felt like the first time
in the arms of a man, I felt safe.
I was still me—the switch was not flicked,
but the terrible feeling haunting me
then didn't reach me.
Which is one of the things that love can feel like.

—Alexander Chee,
from his 2018 collection of essays, How to Write an Autobiographical Novel. *The American fiction writer, poet and journalist is known for his bestselling novels* Edinburgh *and* The Queen of the Night. *Chee was a 2021 Guggenheim Fellow in nonfiction.*

Realising that I might be gay felt like such a relief— I realised I'd never fit in with their straight expectations and it gave me an opportunity to renegotiate being a woman on my own terms.

—Pippa Sterk,
an Indonesian-Dutch writer. Sterk is also a Ph.D. candidate and an ambassador for the charity Just Like Us, which focuses on issues facing LGBTQ+ youth.

MINDFUL MOMENT

I love myself the way I am.

Your queerness is beautiful, and it's a huge reason to love the person you are. It's special, it's pivotal and it's foundational to who you are. Remind yourself as often as you need that you will love yourself in this (and every other) moment.

Sometimes I forget that I'm gay.
Which is to say I sometimes forget that
not everyone is gay and that it is, in some spaces,
an experience of otherness that needs explanation.
My mind palace is a queer utopia.
Like a potluck at a co-op. In some small way,
I always knew that I was gay,
but it's also true that I continue to discover
new aspects of my queer self every day.

—R. Eric Thomas,
an American author, playwright and screenwriter whose essay collection Here for It: Or, How to Save Your Soul in America *(2020) was a finalist for the Lambda Literary Award and was named one of the 10 best books of the year in 2020 by* Teen Vogue *and one of the best books of the year in 2020 by* O: The Oprah Magazine.

We fitted together like the two halves of an oyster-shell. I was Narcissus, embracing the pond in which I was about to drown. However much we had to hide our love, however guarded we had to be about our pleasure, I could not long be miserable about a thing so very sweet. Nor, in my gladness, could I quite believe that anybody would be anything but happy for me if only they knew.

—Sarah Waters,
from her novel Tipping the Velvet *(1998), which features lesbian protagonists in Victorian society. The Welsh novelist is known for her historical queer love stories which also include* Fingersmith *(2002) and* The Night Watch *(2006).*

I wanted to be even more authentic in my music and let people into my life. I'm much more confident now—in my music, myself, my sexuality, the things that I believe that I stand for.

—Lil Nas X,

an American rapper, singer and songwriter. His country rap song "Old Town Road" went viral in 2019, and he followed that up by becoming the most nominated male artist at the 62nd Grammy Awards, at which he won Best Music Video and Best Pop Duo/Group Performance. He is also the first openly LGBTQ+ Black artist to win a Country Music Association Award.

MINDFUL MOMENT

I deserve love and affection from others.

It can be easy to think that if we could just change a few more things about ourselves, or finally be a certain way, or work through a few more of our issues, then we would really deserve love—but that way of thinking is actually what needs to change. Use this refrain to remember that we as queer people are deserving of all the love and affection in the world, right now and with no strings attached.

You were so scared of being bad that it was killing you and now you're really alive, screaming and whining and laughing.... I love that you want to make people feel included because when you were in middle school only two people came to your Hawaiian themed birthday party.... You are so big and bright.... You pay attention to everything and you love God and being bisexual but mostly gay. I like and love all the stuff about you.

—MEG STALTER,

in a letter to herself via Instagram. The American comedian and actor rose to fame through her videos on social media before landing a breakout role on the HBO series Hacks.

Above all else, it is about leaving a mark that I existed: I was here. I was hungry. I was defeated. I was happy. I was sad. I was in love. I was afraid. I was hopeful. I had an idea and I had a good purpose and that's why I made works of art.

—Felix Gonzalez-Torres,
a Cuban-born conceptual artist who lived in New York City. Gonzalez-Torres was involved in many social and political causes as an openly gay man and his work addressed themes such as love and loss, sickness and rejuvenation and gender and sexuality.

I am proud to say that I've done so many great things for the disability community (there is so much more to be done tho [sic]). Over the course of this year I had the absolute honor to know people from all communities that make me me. That being a woman, having a disability, being Dominican, and finally I can add to that magical layer being queer.

—Jillian Mercado,

an American model and actress who appears in the L Word *reboot* Generation Q.

I'M AS GAY AS A DAFFODIL, MY DEAR!

—Freddie Mercury,

the lead vocalist for the band Queen. Mercury is considered one of the greatest singers in the history of rock music. He battled with AIDS for years before coming out publicly only 24 hours before succumbing to complications from the illness in 1991. Five months after his death, a benefit tribute concert was held in London that raised millions of dollars for AIDS research. Both his life and death have continued to raise awareness for the illness.

You have to go the way your blood beats. If you don't live the only life you have, you won't live some other life, you won't live any life at all.

—James Baldwin,

an acclaimed gay writer and civil rights activist. Baldwin is best known for his essays and semi-autobiographical novels that center on race, politics and sexuality.

EVEN IF YOU'RE NOT READY TO LIVE AT YOUR FULL VOLUME, TURN IT UP HALFWAY AND GET THERE.

—Bobby Berk,

an American interior designer and TV personality best known for being the home expert on the Netflix reboot of Queer Eye.

MINDFUL MOMENT

Step by step is the safest way to grow.

It can be hard to remember that loving ourselves doesn't necessarily happen all at once. In choosing to love even just one piece of yourself, you mark the path to loving all the other pieces of yourself as well. Start small if that's what it takes—there's no rush.

I hope you all find yourselves sleeping with someone you love, maybe not all of the time, but a lot of the time. The touch of a foot in the night is sincere.

—Eileen Myles,

from their book, The Importance of Being Iceland. *The American poet and writer has produced more than 20 volumes of poetry, fiction, non-fiction, libretti, plays and performance pieces over the last three decades and has been the recipient of numerous awards and fellowships for their writing including several Lambda Literary Awards and a Guggenheim Fellowship.*

Ah love is bitter and sweet,
but which is more sweet,
the sweetness
or the bitterness?
none has spoken it.

—Hilda Doolittle,

from the book Selected Poems of H.D. *The American-born poet, novelist, translator and essayist's work focused on themes such as mysticism, sapphic love and feminism. Doolittle wrote under the name H.D. for most of her life and cofounded the avant-garde Imagist group of poets in London with Ezra Pound.*

Yet even though I began identifying as a lesbian myself, there were still some remains of negativity that persisted in the back of my mind. And I'm not alone—research by Just Like Us shows that 68% of lesbians say they've delayed coming out because of harmful stereotypes, such as lesbians being "man-hating" and "unattractive." Experiencing lesbian love for the first time changed that for me. Simple things like holding hands with a woman, napping together, and dancing around a kitchen in our PJs together reshaped the negative imagery that school had given me.

—Mara Harris,
a British writer for GAY TIMES *and ambassador for the LGBTQ+ youth charity Just Like Us.*

There can be no love without justice.

—bell hooks,

an American author and social activist. hooks was a distinguished professor in residence at Berea College and is best known for her writings on race, feminism and class. Her most well-known books include Ain't I a Woman *and* All About Love: New Visions.

Love is universal, luckily, but also in general I've found that whenever I've been the most specific in my stand-up, revealing some weird neurosis or quirk I'm ashamed of, that's what people relate to the most.

—Mae Martin,
a Canadian-born comedian who wrote and starred in the semi-autobiographical Netflix series Feel Good.

The rapport between two men or two women can be absolute and perfect, as it can never be between man and woman, and perhaps some people want just this, as others want that more shifting and uncertain thing that happens between men and women.

—Patricia Highsmith,
from her novel The Price of Salt *(1952), which follows the love story of two women in 1950s Manhattan. It was adapted into the film* Carol *(2015). The American novelist and short story writer was widely known for her psychological thrillers, including* Strangers on a Train *(1950) and* The Talented Mr. Ripley *(1955).*

CUT THE ENDING. REVISE THE SCRIPT. THE MAN OF HER DREAMS IS A GIRL.

—Julie Anne Peters,

from her queer YA novel, Keeping You a Secret *(2007).* Luna *(2004) was a National Book Award Finalist and* Between Mom and Jo *(2006) won a Lambda Literary Award.*

I'm queer. But why would people get so upset about something that feels so good?

—Rita Mae Brown,

from her coming-of-age autobiographical novel, Rubyfruit Jungle *(1973). Brown was active in a number of civil rights campaigns and criticized the marginalization of lesbians within feminist groups. She received the Pioneer Award at the Lambda Literary Awards in 2015.*

I learned compassion from being discriminated against. Everything bad that's ever happened to me has taught me compassion.

—Ellen DeGeneres,

an American television host, comedian, writer and producer. DeGeneres got her start in stand-up comedy and her life as a comedian became the basis for her 1990s sitcom, Ellen. *She came out publicly as a lesbian in 1997, after which she felt her career was stunted due to public and industry backlash. Six years later, however, she went on to host her own talk show,* The Ellen DeGeneres Show, *which ran from 2003 to 2022 and received numerous awards.*

MINDFUL MOMENT

I lovingly nurture my mind, body and spirit.

This will look different from day to day, but use this affirmation to remind yourself to tune in to whatever your current needs are. Sit in the sun, pick a flower, write a letter, read a book—whatever feels good. Note that this affirmation has the important addition of "lovingly," which might seem small, but isn't. Choosing to nurture ourselves from a place of love makes such a difference. It's a tough world out there; we need all the love we can get.

Your female crushes were always floating past you, out of reach, but she touches your arm and looks directly at you and you feel like a child buying something with her own money for the first time.

—Carmen Maria Machado,

from her memoir, In The Dream House *(2019). The book chronicles the abusive relationship with her ex-girlfriend and was awarded the 2021 Folio Prize and the 2020 Lambda Literary Award for LGBTQ Nonfiction.*

As I sat there waiting to walk, I was feeling this great sense of pride thinking about my journey to this moment, the only Latina in this massive show, excited to be a part of something so amazing. Gaultier was a genius but he was also doing exactly what he wanted to do. It made me realize that I could be myself, too. That was the moment, I decided right there. It all just clicked suddenly.

—Patricia Velasquez,

from her 2015 memoir, Straight Walk: A Supermodel's Journey to Finding Her Truth. *The book served as Velasquez's official public coming out. The Venezuelan model and actress is known for her role in* The Mummy *(1999).*

I want you to know that the courage it takes to be honest with your true self is something I know too. Coming out is hard for all of us, but it's even harder when you have to do it from the standpoint of being a hero for other people.

—Eve May,

a trans teen who rose to fame after writing a heartfelt letter to Lil Nas X in Teen Vogue *in 2022. That year, May was voted one of GLAAD's 20 under 20 Outstanding Young LGBTQ Changemakers.*

MY EXISTENCE HOLDS A SPECIAL PLACE IN THIS WORLD. THERE IS ONLY ONE ME.

—Zuriel Hooks,

a content creator and activist known for her work for The Knights and Orchids Society, a nonprofit that provides free health care for Black LGBTQ+ people in Alabama.

For us growing up, we never got to experience seeing two Black men in love, visually, on a big screen. It was just something we didn't see. We knew it existed but we just didn't see it.

—Jason Bolden,

an American creative director, fashion stylist and interior designer. He and his husband Adair Curtis cofounded JSN Studio, and their Netflix series Styling Hollywood *follows them as they style their celebrity clients.*

I love it. I feel happier and more content with what I have and who I am, and less—what's the word? Covetous. The older I get, the more I embrace who I am.

—K.D. Lang,

a Canadian pop and country singer-songwriter, on getting older. Her most successful song was "If I Were You" (1995) and she is also considered one of pop culture's biggest lesbian heartthrobs of the '90s.

MINDFUL MOMENT

I honor my heart, my loving energy and my true self.

Loving is all about honesty and vulnerability, but when the outside world misconstrues softness as weakness, it's hard not to take that to heart. When that happens, use this affirmation to remember to honor your sweet, loving self.

I identify as trans, nonbinary, and trans-masculine, and I use he and they pronouns. I feel that for me the journey of transness is about reclaiming our ancient heritage. We have always existed. In cultures around the world, the ancient ways included and usually uplifted the value of trans people.

—Daniel Sea,

an American actor who portrayed the first recurring transmasculine character in the original L Word. *His character, Max, returned for the 2019 sequel series* The L Word: Generation Q.

I'm not crazy for feeling this way. They're crazy for trying to stop me. And if t's the last time I ever get to feel joy again, I won't let them have it.

—JAMES BRANDON,
from his queer YA novel, Ziggy, Stardust and Me *(2019). Brandon is also an actor and producer.*

LOVE HAS NO GENDER—COMPASSION HAS NO RELIGION—CHARACTER HAS NO RACE.

—ABHIJIT NASKAR,
from his book, Either Civilized or Phobic: A Treatise on Homosexuality *(2017), which delves into the neuroscience of sexuality. Naskar is known for using his research to further humanitarian causes globally.*

MINDFUL MOMENT

I am aligned with the highest frequency of love.

You might be used to others questioning the way you love or who you love, which can cause you to question yourself. As queer folks, we have this capacity to love in ways that many straight folks might not understand—and that's a beautiful thing. Use this affirmation to remind yourself of the high vibration you actually radiate on.

Love isn't just a matter of looking at someone, I think now, but also of looking with them, of facing what they face.

—GARTH GREENWELL,

from his book, What Belongs to You *(2016), which* The New Republic *called "the Great Gay Novel for our times."*

Two women in love confirms for me that there is a love that can push you beyond what everyone else says is possible.

—DAISY HERNÁNDEZ,

from her 2014 memoir A Cup of Water Under My Bed, *which chronicles what it was like growing up queer in a Columbian-Cuban family. Hernández is an intersectional feminist author and journalist who writes about race, immigration and queer/bisexual life.*

As I pondered a pronoun change,
I began to think of gender less as a scale
and more as a landscape.
Some people are born in the mountains,
while others are born by the sea.
Some people are happy to live in the place
they were born, while others must make
a journey to reach the climate
in which they can flourish and grow.
Between the ocean and
the mountains is a wild forest.
That is where I want to make my home.

—Maia Kobabe,
from their 2019 memoir, Gender Queer. *Due to its prominent LGBTQ+ themes, the book was listed as 2021's most challenged graphic novel by The American Library Association's Office of Intellectual Freedom, having been banned or opposed by several schools and libraries. In 2022, the book placed first on PEN America's annual list of the top banned titles of the year.*

Our community exists because of our tireless fight for visibility, and because of that, our community is strong. Lean into this collective of love and draw from it your birthright: queer power.

—Zander Moricz,
an activist known for fighting Florida's "Parental Rights in Education" bill (also known as the "Don't Say Gay" bill) who became the youngest plaintiff in the lawsuit against the state.

I was falling in love with my best friend and instead of being able to do anything about it, I watched him fall in love with someone else because I didn't have the courage to act publicly on my feelings.... I was missing out on the good stuff because I was walking around with an invisible rain cloud over my head, smiling through the heartbreak so as to avoid anyone asking me what was wrong—because I didn't have the strength to tell them.

—Dan Levy,

while accepting the Davidson/Valentini Award at the GLAAD Gala San Francisco in 2019. Levy, an actor and writer, is the creator of the show Schitt's Creek, *which is celebrated by the LGBTQ+ community for its representation of a queer relationship that is fully accepted by all other characters.*

I was not ladylike, nor was I manly. I was something else altogether. There were so many different ways to be beautiful.

—Michael Cunningham,
from his novel, A Home at the End of the World *(1990).*
He is best known for his 1998 novel The Hours,
which won the Pulitzer Prize for Fiction and the PEN/Faulkner Award in 1999.

I am open to love in all forms.

Being queer means there's so much more room for experimentation, as we already exist outside of the norm. Embrace that. Our world has told us again and again what love is supposed to look like (straight, monogamous, cis, etc.) and how it should feel, and it's up to us as queer folks to choose to reject those ideas every day. Remember, love can take many shapes—enjoy the exploration.

For trans and nonbinary youth: You're beautiful. You're important. You're valid. You're perfect.

—Kacen Callender,

in the dedication to his queer YA novel, Felix Ever After *(2020). The American writer's debut children's novel,* Hurricane Child *(2018), earned them a Stonewall Book Award and a Lambda Literary Award.*

I didn't come in here with the mission, "I'm going to make the Polish queer population proud by going on this show." But I'm out there talking about my personal life, fluidity and what it's like to be in a gay relationship on this show. That takes vulnerability and maybe that is something to be proud of.

—Antoni Porowski,

a Canadian television personality, cook, model, author and the food and wine expert on the Netflix series Queer Eye.

MINDFUL MOMENT

I love each part of myself.

That means the messy parts, the wild parts, the soft parts, the quiet parts, the parts that you were told to hide away. Now is the time to say yes, I love all of these pieces of me.

I can meet a man tomorrow and fall in love with him and marry him and I wouldn't discount any of the experiences that I've had with women, or vice versa. I just don't think anyone is in a position to dictate what that is for me.

—Sarah Paulson,
an American actress known for her various roles in the anthology series American Horror Story.

[Don't] be scared of yourself. You will never find happiness in other people.

—Jade LeMac,
an Asian musician who was one of GLAAD's 20 under 20 Outstanding Young LGBTQ Changemakers in 2022.

If you are on the fence and if you are in doubt and you are afraid, take that step and really reach out. And honesty and mental health and confidence all should be folded in together.

—Sandra Bernhard,

an American comedian, actress, author and singer. Bernhard is known for her work on American Horror Story, Pose *and* Roseanne*—a series in which she portrayed one of the first recurring lesbian characters in television history.*

TO LOVE ONESELF IS THE BEGINNING OF A LIFE-LONG ROMANCE.

—Oscar Wilde,

a celebrated Irish poet, novelist and playwright. He's best known for his only novel, The Picture of Dorian Gray *(1891), and his play* The Importance of Being Earnest *(1895). Near the end of his life, Wilde was imprisoned for engaging in homosexual acts, which were deemed criminal at the time, and was incarcerated in London from 1895 to 1897.*

My work has become a reflection of the self-love I discovered through Lady Gaga's lyrics; I can now reclaim my queerness and help others do the same.

—Javier Gomez,

an American activist. While still in high school, Gomez fought Florida's "Don't Say Gay" bill and even spoke as part of President Biden's Pride Month Celebration in June 2022.

I just remember this moment where I'm at this stop sign and I'm sitting there and it just really hit me that the one person in the world that I thought would love me no matter what, I just lost that person. In that moment I had this weird feeling of strength because, in that moment I remember thinking: that's not entirely true, you still have one other person and that person's you.

—Alice Wu,
a Chinese-American writer and director whose films Saving Face *(2004) and* The Half of It *(2020) focus on queer female protagonists.*

MINDFUL MOMENT

I am love.

It's also worth remembering that love is something we can embody—it's not necessarily something that relies on the presence of others. We don't have to look for it, ask for it or wait for it—we are love.

TWO DUDES MET. THEY FELL IN LOVE. THEY LIVED. THAT'S OUR STORY.

—Adam Silvera,
from his queer YA novel, They Both Die at the End *(2017). His other bestselling YA novels include* More Happy Than Not *(2015) and* History Is All You Left Me *(2017).*

If there were to be anything close to what I feel it would be pan. I accept love in all forms and I give love. It's just all love.

—Arienne Mandi,
an American actress who stars on The L Word: Generation Q.

The beautiful shades of the world are the colors of love that pour out from the light within us all.

—Karamo Brown,

from his memoir, Karamo: My Story of Embracing Purpose, Healing, and Hope *(2019). Brown is a reality television personality, author and activist. Brown was the first openly gay Black man cast on a reality show when he appeared on* The Real World: Philadelphia *in 2004. He later rose to greater fame as a member of the Fab Five on the 2018 reboot of* Queer Eye.

It's been tough and uncomfortable at times, but it has given me the confidence to be myself, to follow my own path, and to rise above adversity and bigotry. It's also given me the skin of a rhinoceros, which comes in handy when you're the CEO of Apple.... So let me be clear: I'm proud to be gay, and I consider being gay among the greatest gifts God has given me.

—Tim Cook,

the CEO of Apple. Cook publicly came out in 2014 after much speculation about his sexuality.

This film is not gay, it's life. We never talk about heterosexual films. "Oh, I saw this great heterosexual love story." For me, it's not a story of homosexuality or gay love—it's love.

—Xavier Dolan,

a Canadian filmmaker and actor speaking about his film Matthias & Maxime *(2019). He's also known for his films* I Killed My Mother *(2009) and* Mommy *(2014). He has won several awards at the Cannes Film Festival including the Jury Prize and the Grand Prix.*

People don't realize that I've spent my whole life seeing other people getting to have their love stories [on screen] but never somebody who represented what me and my friends have gone through.

—Greg Berlanti,

an American director and TV showrunner who directed Love, Simon *(2018), which is considered to be one of the first teen movies centered on gay romance from a major studio.*

My queerness is beautiful.

It's not just that your queerness is a part of you, it's one of the best parts of you. Use this affirmation to elevate your perception of what your queerness is. The more you can embrace your queerness fully, the more self-love you'll have toward your identity.

If you can't love yourself, how in the hell you gonna love somebody else?

—RuPaul,

an American drag queen, television personality, actor, musician and model. best known for hosting, producing and judging the reality competition RuPaul's Drag Race, *which has had a huge impact on bringing drag into the mainstream. The cultural effect of the show has sparked shifts in the beauty industry, launched a new wave of memes and GIFs via social media and has even changed the way we speak, popularizing terms like "shade," "sickening" and "fierce."*

Acceptance & Persistence

Once you embrace your true identity, hold on tight as you continue your journey.

Nature made a mistake, which I have corrected, and I am now your daughter.

—Christine Jorgensen,

from her book, Christine Jorgensen: A Personal Autobiography *(1967). She was an actress and singer and is considered to be one of America's first transgender celebrities after news of her gender affirmation surgery was leaked to the press in the 1950s.*

I waited *forever* to come out because that's what people kept saying to me, that [being bisexual] was a "phase." Guess what? I'm still bisexual.

—Lucy LaForge,

lead singer-songwriter of the indie pop band Lucy & La Mer.

My parents have always been super supportive. My sister and I have always been really close and she's been really supportive as with my brother. When it was time to come out, I was obviously scared, as most people are. After I got all the love and support from my family then I knew I could go out and conquer the world, I guess.

—EJ Johnson,

an American television personality, socialite and son of Magic Johnson. In 2013, after his sexual orientation was leaked in the press, Johnson decided to come out publicly himself.

MINDFUL MOMENT

I am queer enough.

There may be times when it feels overwhelming to step into this potentially new identity. But no matter how long you've been a part of the queer community, it's important to remember that there's no need to earn your place here or prove yourself in any particular way. All who feel they belong are welcome.

I knew right once I saw her, like, "Whoa, she's really pretty, and I really like her." But I was just thinking, "Oh, like a friend." As we became best friends, I was like, "Mmm, I don't think it's that..." I couldn't avoid my feelings.

—JoJo Siwa,

an American dancer, singer and YouTube star. Her social media reach spans millions of followers between Instagram and YouTube, and in 2020, Time *named her one of its 100 Most Influential People.*

Most people think the closet is a small room. They think you can touch the walls, touch the door, turn the handle, and walk free. But when you're inside it, the closet is vast. No walls, no door, just empty darkness stretching the length of the world.

—S.J. Sindu,

from her first novel, Marriage of a Thousand Lies *(2017), which won the Publishing Triangle Edmund White Award and was also a Stonewall Honor Book and a finalist for a Lambda Literary Award. The Tamil diaspora author has also published another novel and two chapbooks.*

I don't know what happens now, and that's alrite. I don't have any secrets I need kept anymore.... I feel like a free man.

—Frank Ocean,

an American singer, songwriter and rapper known for his introspective lyrics and avant-garde style. Ocean came out publicly via a letter posted to his Tumblr page in 2012. The letter speaks openly and honestly about his sexual fluidity and helped to shift the landscape for other young queer Black hip-hop artists.

I really want people to realize there's not one perfect way to be queer. I think we realize this as we get older, but even with the way people talk about these things online, it may seem like there are boxes to check off or a test to pass and there simply aren't. It's OK if you call yourself a lesbian even if you haven't been with any women yet. It's OK if you identify as one thing for a few years and then change your mind. Plus, your sexuality can be specific to you, and that's OK!

—Camryn Garrett,
an American writer and filmmaker known for her novels Full Disclosure *(2019) and* Off the Record (2021) *and her short film* Underwater *(2016).*

It's just magic. I love how much being trans makes me think outside the box in every part of my life, because I don't fit neatly into any category. And I love how what makes being trans hard is also what can make it beautiful, how being trans and nonbinary means existing outside of everything. It gives me such a unique perspective on being free.

—Layshia Clarendon,
the first openly nonbinary and transgender player in the WNBA.

Queer is a word whose usage I continue to follow. It was chosen because in a world where people are groomed to be *normal* and rewarded for it, a queer person is an alien, an un-belonger, *strange* and therefore a threat. It was a smart move to choose that word; but a smart thing can be outsmarted, which is how even though I know what it *used* to mean, I can also clearly see how far it has traveled in order to mean the freeing thing it does to me now.

—Eloghosa Osunde,

a Nigerian writer and artist. Her novel Vagabonds *(2022), set in a society where same-sex romance is illegal, was longlisted for the Center for Fiction's First Novel Prize, shortlisted for the Waterstones Debut Fiction Prize and was named a "Most Anticipated Book of The Year" by* The New Yorker, L.A. Times *and* The New York Times.

I came into my sexuality super late, though you can come out even if you're way older than I was....In terms of finding yourself as a full-grown adult, realizing that the world is way bigger than what you thought and realizing that there's so much more to know about yourself? I really resonate with that.

—Abbi Jacobson,

an American comedian, actress, writer and producer. She's best known for the Comedy Central show she cowrote and starred in, Broad City, *which was based on the web series she created with costar Ilana Glazer.*

MINDFUL MOMENT

The people who deserve to love me will be excited to accept the real me.

Anyone we give our time and energy to should be someone who values us for who we are—and that very much includes our queerness. This goes beyond romantic relationships as well (of course, those folks should also be excited and eager to accept the real you). Use this simple reminder as often as you need.

**When I started getting older,
I started realizing
how queer I really am.
This past year
I was engaged to a man,
and when it didn't work,
I was like,
"This is a huge sign."
I thought I was going to
spend my life with someone.
Now that I wasn't going to,
I felt this sense of relief
that I could live my truth.**

—DEMI LOVATO,

an American actor, singer and pop star. After a successful run as a child actor on Disney Channel, Lovato released their first album in 2008. They've gone on to become one of the most successful recording artists of their generation, achieving such accolades as an MTV Video Music Award, 14 Teen Choice Awards, five People's Choice Awards and an ALMA Award.

THERE'S NOTHING WRONG WITH YOU. THERE'S A LOT WRONG WITH THE WORLD YOU LIVE IN.

—Chris Colfer,
an American singer, actor and author. Colfer is known for his portrayal of Kurt Hummel on Glee.

If I didn't have a clear understanding of who I was yet, then I wouldn't have anything meaningful to say. And I think it's important for people to come out, but it's far more important to come out in your own time, because otherwise you're doing it for someone else's benefit and not your own, and then what is there to be said?

—Kate Moennig,
an American actress known for her role as Shane McCutcheon on HBO's The L Word. *She resumed the role for the reboot,* The L Word: Generation Q, *(2019).*

I think queer women aren't afraid to be who they are and don't care about fitting into a particular box that society dictates for us. And for many queer women, being masculine and athletic is natural to our existence and when it comes to sports, that's an asset. I think sports and teams in general are safe spaces for queer folks, because being athletic for women was already subverting societal norms.

—Lyndsey D'Arcangelo,
the former Editor-in-Chief of Curve *magazine from 2010 to 2020 and coauthor of the 2021 book* Hail Mary: The Rise and Fall of the National Women's Football League.

They weren't ready for a controversial real take on gay culture that tapped into some really heavy, dark shit about trauma. [The TV show] didn't happen, and now I'm known for doing one-minute videos on the internet. That's what life is right now, and then it'll evolve into something else. And maybe then I'll feel completely seen, but probably not then either. It's a never-ending journey.

—Jordan Firstman,
an American comedian and actor who achieved viral fame with his Instagram impressions during the early stages of lockdown and quarantine of the COVID-19 pandemic. He was previously a writer on the shows Search Party *and* Big Mouth.

For a lot of my life, I was judged for my gender representation or my sexual orientation, or what people assumed of me; and every single time my goal has been to combat that and show my greatness.

—Taylor Small,

an American politician. In 2020, she was elected to the Vermont House of Representatives, making her the first openly transgender member of the Vermont Legislature.

MINDFUL MOMENT

I don't need others to understand me in order to understand myself.

There are going to be times (many, perhaps) when you're not feeling understood by others. Maybe there are parts of you that don't make sense to these people, maybe you make them question aspects of the world they'd rather not—whatever the case may be, remember that whether anyone else understands you or not, you understand yourself. And that's what truly matters.

Recently I've found myself wondering why and how my brain had been programmed to ignore an attraction that in retrospect seems so evident to me. I believe it was all just a matter of chemistry that had nothing to do with gender. I still don't feel like I'm in a place to label my sexuality one way or another, but I'm OK with that. It's something I'm still exploring and figuring out.... Even I don't entirely understand what my experience this summer means for me going forward— and it's *my* experience.

—Kaitlynn Carter,

an American model and television personality. She was famously engaged to American model Brody Jenner, and, post-split, wrote an essay about her summer romance with Miley Cyrus. Although she wrote openly about her experience, Carter refused to label her sexuality.

Shame was a place where many of my lessons came from, and so part of the great freedom of my adult life has been doing away with shame little by little and sometimes abundantly at a time. Even when I don't feel bright and alive... like, I want to be shamelessly depressed! I want to be shamelessly Black, gay, unapologetically neurodivergent, you know? If there is one tool people can cull from my poems, it's that shame is one of the best unburdenings you can do.

—Danez Smith,
an American poet. Their book Don't Call Us Dead *(2017) was a finalist for the National Book Award. Their 2014 book* [insert] boy *won the Lambda Literary Award. Smith is also a 2011 Individual World Poetry Slam finalist.*

Transition and coming out can and should be a spiritual experience, as well as an emotional and social and sometimes physical one. There is something beautiful about growing into who we were created to be and growing into our authentic selves.

—Bingo Allison,
the Church of England's first nonbinary priest.

I knew my coming out would be important and significant. It was a message. It was going to let lesbians all over the world know they are not alone.

—Alix Dobkin,

an American folk singer, songwriter and lesbian activist. She was active in the New York folk scene of the 1960s and her debut record, Lavender Jane Loves Women *(1973), is considered one of the first lesbian albums.*

There are those from religious backgrounds who resist and oppose LGBT equality; some very obsessively and publicly. They make bold accusations and negative statements about gay and lesbian people, their supposed "lifestyle" and relationships. But when a son, daughter, brother, sister or close friend comes out it is no longer an "issue," it becomes a person. They realize everything they'd said was painfully targeted at someone they love.

—Anthony Venn-Brown,
a former Australian evangelist who went on to write about his experience of trying to reconcile his homosexuality with his Christian beliefs in the book A Life of Unlearning *(2004).*

What I feel we have arrived at with all this, is that queerness—as I am happy to call an all-embracing, foundational tenet—is really a state of mind brought about by an understanding: It is understanding difference, accepting your own truth, desire and identity, and lovely, lovely choice.

—MICHAEL STIPE,
the lead singer of the band R.E.M.

I HAVE A HOMOSEXUAL SON AND I LOVE HIM.

—JEANNE MANFORD,
on her son Morty Manford in a 1972 letter to the editor in The New York Post. *Manford was a cofounder of the organization POG (Parents of Gays), which later became PFLAG (Parents, Family and Friends of Lesbians and Gays).*

It was very much a feeling of relief for me, because Lou Dobbs is clearly one of the most important people in my life. Almost, clearly a brother figure. He's a western cowboy, a macho homophobe, who was really a very good friend of mine. And I was afraid of what his reaction would be.... He totally surprised me. I did not have any negative reaction from him. He said, "What do you want me to do?" He said, "Do you want me to tell anybody or do you want me not to tell anybody?" I said, "I think you better tell everyone." I was tired. I was tired of living a lie.

—Tom Cassidy,
an American television journalist who anchored CNN's show Pinnacle *from 1984 to 1988. Cassidy helped raise awareness for HIV and AIDS by speaking publicly about his treatment and progress after being diagnosed in 1987.*

It doesn't inspire young men and women struggling with their own sexuality to be confident in who they are if I'm not confident in who I am. And if I whisper about it, then I give other people the power to whisper about it, and there's nothing wrong with it. I definitely want to get louder.

—Gavin Creel,
an American actor who's appeared in Broadway productions of Hello, Dolly! *(for which he received a Tony Award),* Hair *(Tony nomination),* La Cage aux Folles, She Loves Me, The Book of Mormon *and* Waitress.

MINDFUL MOMENT

If who I am makes others uncomfortable, that says more about them than it does about me.

Whatever the situation may be, whomever it involves, whatever feelings it brings up—if you and your queerness cause discomfort for others, that's their problem. At the core is a lack of understanding on their part, which you shouldn't feel obligated to accommodate.

I've never felt any reason to hide. When you're self-conscious about anything—your appearance, your age, your sexuality—it tends to be the first thing people notice. Everybody is a little self-conscious; it's what makes us human. If you accept who you are and achieve the level of comfort to own it and embrace it, people will allow you to be you. I've never hidden behind a façade, and because of that people have celebrated me for being the great swimmer that I was.

—Amini Fonua,

a Tongan swimmer who was one of only 56 openly gay athletes to compete at the 2016 Summer Olympics. Fonua has used his platform to speak about queer rights as homosexuality is still a punishable crime in his home country.

WHAT DIDN'T YOU DO TO BURY ME/ BUT YOU FORGOT THAT I WAS A SEED

—Dinos Christianopoulos,

a Greek poet. While he felt ostracized by the Greek literary world of the 1970s, this couplet (and slight variations of it) has gone on to resonate with protestors worldwide, being used by Mexican activists as recently as 2013.

What do you think gay people do? Have done for generations? We adopt a safe version of ourselves for the public, for protection, and then as adults we excavate our true selves from the parts we've invented to protect us. It's the most important work of queer lives.

—Steven Rowley,

an American author whose bestselling book Lily and the Octopus *(2016) was a* Washington Post *Notable Book in 2016. His novel* The Editor *was named one of the Best Books of 2019 by NPR and* Esquire, *and his 2021 book* The Guncle *was a Goodreads Choice Awards finalist for Novel of the Year.*

MINDFUL MOMENT

I have compassion for myself and others.

Acceptance means treating ourselves with kindness and empathy (yes, you can empathize with yourself, and you should). Compassion is at the root of understanding. Remind yourself of this when you feel out of place or when people are frustrating you. The more kindness we have for ourselves, the more kindness we can have for those around us.

**The body is the only thing you really own.
I own my brain, I own my biceps, my knees, my toes.
I didn't pick it, it was assigned to me somehow;
I don't think I asked for this particular configuration.
I look in the mirror and think,
"This is just how I turned out looking."
I didn't necessarily ask to be white or male
or transgender, it's the package that I'm in.
I like the sense of weirdness that this perspective generates,
because it's not a comfortable way of approaching life,
to have this abstraction of who you are.**

—Pippa Garner,
an American artist known for her drawings, performances and satirical consumer product inventions, which include the Hurl-a-Burger, a small catapult machine designed to launch food over border walls, and "Luv-Cuffs," which would replace couples therapy by binding a couple together for 24 hours. She was an advocate for gender fluidity back in the 1980s and has described her own transition to female as an "act of artistic expression."

I think that part of the reason I'm being more vocal is I spent a while trying to figure out how that would work. Part of my thinking is that I was raised in a conservative environment. I always say I can sympathize with people who are transphobic because I used to be transphobic, and I know where they're coming from.

—Amy Schneider,
a transgender lesbian American writer and television personality known for her epic 40-episode winning streak on Jeopardy!*, the second-longest in the show's history. Schneider is also the first trans woman to qualify for the show's* Tournament of Champions.

When I told [my mom] that I thought I might be a lesbian... She didn't say a whole lot. She kind of got teary-eyed and then she said, "Well, you know, maybe you should see a psychiatrist." What seems natural is to follow my own instincts and my desires.... The only natural thing for me is what I've been feeling since day one in the world. And why would I try to change that? How foolish I've been!... It was like a light going off in my head that his argument—in terms of what is natural—really does make sense, but you have to know what's natural for you.

—Rev. Carolyn Mobley-Bowie,
a reverend who has worked with the LGBTQ+-affirming Metropolitan Community Church. In the 1980s, she was also a founding member of the African American Lesbian Gay Alliance (AALGA).

The first group of LGBTQ people to embrace me, at 16, was the drag community. There was a little bar called Martha's Vineyard and at one point I was doing drag. This was before cellphones. That's where I found the most acceptance and love. I eventually moved around a lot, but I'm lucky to have found my chosen family—and a lot of allies.

—Bobby Berk,
an American interior designer and TV personality best known for being the home expert on the reboot of Queer Eye.

Anytime one tries to take fragments of one's personal mythology and make them understandable to the whole world, one reaches back to the past. It must be dreamed again.

—Assotto Saint,

a Haitian poet and writer who was an active member of the LGBTQ+ and African American literary scenes of New York City in the 1980s and early 1990s.

My gender has always been very fluid. Someone would call me "she" or "her" and I wouldn't think about it, but I knew that if someone called me "he" it was a bit exciting.

—Bella Ramsey,
a British actor best known for their roles in the HBO series Game of Thrones *and* The Last of Us. *They came out publicly as nonbinary via an interview with* The New York Times *in January 2023.*

I had never seen someone like Shane, who's not super femme, so for me I was like, "Oh, wow, there are other women—it's not just this bombshell blonde that is in heels and a dress." I didn't feel like I fit that mold.

—JACQUELINE TOBONI,
on watching The L Word. *The American actress is known for her role on the show* Grimm. *In 2019, she joined the cast of* The L Word: Generation Q.

When I started to come into my sexuality, I was around 19 or 20 years old—and I'm only 22 now. So part of me did almost feel like, "I'm too late, I should have known this about myself," and so I wasn't validating myself and I was questioning myself all the time... until I started talking to people who had similar experiences to me... The timing of when you realize [it] isn't important, it's about the celebration and being able to embrace it. That's what matters.

—REBECCA BLACK,
an American singer and YouTuber who came to fame with her viral song "Friday" in 2011.

I didn't know why it made my heart sing loud to itself that a stranger thought I was a boy. It just did. Made me feel like he could look inside me and see some part of the truth of me in there. But it did make me inexplicably sad that a stranger could see me, and my own family could not.

—Ivan E. Coyote,
from their memoir, Tomboy Survival Guide *(2016), which chronicles growing up as a tomboy in the Canadian Yukon and is a 2017 Stonewall Honor Book.*

MINDFUL MOMENT

I accept my sexuality as a gift.

Every day is a chance to embrace your sexuality as a gift—not as a burden to overcome, not as something to be tolerated, not as something that sets you apart. If you can view your sexuality as a gift, life can move and shift in some beautiful ways.

Coming out is not an easy thing to do no matter who you are, no matter where you come from. We all have the opportunity to reach the other side and still deserve to be loved and deserve to be accepted and even if the people around us don't always handle it exactly the right way immediately, it doesn't mean that they can't also grow and that they can't also change.

—Clea DuVall,
an actor and director of the Hulu lesbian holiday romcom Happiest Season *(2020).*

Right before the issue was released, I had a purging of all the fear and toxicity that had accumulated over my entire life. I literally wound up in the emergency room, thinking I was having a heart attack.

—Tyler Glenn,
a musician, on coming out in Rolling Stone *in 2014. Glenn is the front man of the band Neon Trees.*

Never be bullied into silence. Never allow yourself to be made a victim. Accept no one's definition of your life, but define yourself.

—Harvey Fierstein,

a playwright, actor and Tony winner.
He's known for his roles in the movies Mrs. Doubtfire *(1993) and* Independence Day *(1996), as well as for writing the groundbreaking play* Torch Song Trilogy, *which focuses on gay families and was later adapted into a feature film in 1988.*

Once I understood my gender more, which was unassigned, then I understood my sexuality more. I was like, "Oh—that's why I don't feel straight and I don't feel gay. It's because I'm not."

—MILEY CYRUS,

an American singer, songwriter and actress. The daughter of Billy Ray Cyrus got her start on Disney Channel and has made the successful transition to full-fledged music star with eight studio albums ranging from country to pop to rock to hip-hop. Throughout her career, Cyrus has been a vocal supporter of the LGBTQ+ community, having publicly come out as both pansexual and genderfluid.

I was called every name in the book. And as well, it wasn't just because I danced, it was because I was different. It's because I was a little bit of feminine. It's because I wasn't like a normal kid, or a normal boy around the block kind of thing. And I've come to terms with the experience it was, but it's also formed me into the person and made me the dancer I became.

—David Hallberg,

a ballet dancer who became the eighth Artistic Director of the Australian Ballet in 2021.

I WILL CREATE MY LIFE—NOT JUST ACCEPT IT.

—Lorraine Hansberry,

an American playwright, writer, lesbian and activist best known for A Raisin in the Sun, *which was the first play by a Black woman produced on Broadway when it opened in 1959.*

MINDFUL MOMENT

With each day that passes, I heal more and more.

Not everyone receives the love and acceptance they deserve when they first open up about their sexuality and/or gender identity. If you had to endure a painful period, this affirmation is for you. Remember that healing is a process, and it happens a little bit at a time.

I was forcing myself and shoving myself into a box that didn't fit me, and I was causing myself so much pain and trauma just trying endlessly to be something that I wasn't because that's all I thought I could be. We talk so much about the boxes society puts us in as queer people and the boxes that the world puts us in and bullies put us in and blah blah blah, but we never talk about the boxes we put ourselves in... I didn't realize that the pain being inflicted wasn't inherently societal; it was self-inflicted.

—Lachlan Watson,

an American actor best known for playing the trans boy Theo Putnam in the Netflix series Chilling Adventures of Sabrina.

I don't feel like a liar anymore. I've been using the word "sturdy" a lot lately. Like, I feel sturdy. I think I'm accepting a lot of things in my life and not fighting it anymore.

—Jerrod Carmichael,
an American comedian, actor, writer and filmmaker who came out publicly via his 2022 HBO comedy special, Rothaniel.

I grew up in an old-fashioned, repressed English family. And I used the word "gay" to describe things...I think that came from the fact that I just didn't want to admit who I was. I didn't want to upset my family. I was deeply unhappy and depressed. When you don't accept a part of yourself or love yourself, it's like you're not there, almost.

—CARA DELEVIGNE,

a British model and actress. As a model, she was known for being the face of Chanel, and since shifting to acting, she's appeared in the films Anna Karenina *(2012),* Paper Towns *(2015),* Suicide Squad *(2016),* Valerian and the City of a Thousand Planets *(2017) and* Her Smell *(2018).*

DON'T EVER LET ANYONE PUT YOU DOWN BECAUSE YOU'RE GAY.

—JEAN DEVENTE,

an American gay rights activist. She took on much of the organizational work that was required to keep Christopher Street Liberation Day—New York City's Gay Pride—going, even serving as Grand Marshal for the city's first Gay Pride Parade. She's often referred to as the mother of the modern gay rights movement.

I added a rainbow to my name when I felt ready a few years ago, as it's not easy within the south Asian [sic] community to be accepted, and I always answered honestly if ever straight-up asked about it on Twitter. But I kept it low because I was scared of the pain of being accused of performative bandwagon jumping, over something that caused me a lot of confusion, fear and turmoil when I was a kid. I didn't come from a family with anyone openly out. It's also scary as an actor to openly admit your sexuality, especially when you're a brown female in your 30s.

—Jameela Jamil,
a British actress known for TV series such as The Good Place. *Jamil came out publicly after receiving social media backlash for her appointment as a judge on the voguing reality show* Legendary.

MINDFUL MOMENT

I forgive myself.

For some of us, coming to a place of acceptance with our identity likely involved some missteps, times when we didn't know what to do or say or moments we wish we could redo. This is your reminder to let all of that go—missteps are normal and mistakes are what make us human. Choose today as the time to forgive yourself.

I remember my dad saying that he had prayed a lot that his suspicions were wrong. And then we went on to talk and it was kind of teary. But he really opened up and he talked a great deal. And I was surprised. And he even said that if they called him he would talk to them on the telephone, which stunned me.

—Greg Brock,
a news reporter, on coming out to his father and stepmother the day before appearing on Oprah *as part of the first-ever National Coming Out Day in 1988. At the time, Brock was the highest level openly gay person working at a mainstream newspaper anywhere in the United States.*

I'M JUST MORE COMFORTABLE WITH MYSELF NOW. IT'S TAKEN ME UNTIL I'M 42 TO BEGIN TO FEEL THIS WAY.

—Mo Rocca,
a comedian, author and TV personality. Rocca is a correspondent for CBS's Sunday Morning *and the host and creator of* My Grandmother's Ravioli *on the Cooking Channel.*

I really felt that I had to present as a woman in order to find success in this industry. It wasn't sustainable, and I stopped pretending. And weirdly at that point I got nominated for Best Actress for the Golden Globes, which is like, beautifully ironic.... The space for trans people and gender non-conforming people is getting bigger all the time.

—Emma D'Arcy,
a British actor known for their role as Rhaenyra Targaryen in House of the Dragon, *a* Game of Thrones *prequel.*

You can become anything and do anything, right here, right now. It won't be questioned. I came. I saw. I conquered. That's a ball.

—Pepper LaBeija,

an American drag queen who was famously portrayed in the 1990 documentary Paris Is Burning. *She was known as the last remaining queen of the Harlem drag balls.*

I say that it is time to open the closet door and let in the fresh air and the sunshine; time to discard the secrecy, the disguise, and the camouflage; time to hold up your heads and look the world squarely in the eye... confident of your equality, confident in the knowledge that as objects of prejudice and victims of discrimination, you are right and they are wrong, and confident of the rightness of what you are and the goodness of what you do; it is time to live your homosexuality fully, joyously, openly, and proudly, assured that morally, socially, physically, psychologically, emotionally, and in every other way: Gay is Good.

—Frank Kameny,

an American gay rights activist who is considered one of the most significant figures in the movement. Kameny worked to bring the homophile movement into the streets in the mid-1960s, led the fight to remove homosexuality from the APA's list of mental disorders, fought many of the government's anti-gay policies and most notably coined the phrase "Gay is Good" (which is based on the phrase "Black is Beautiful").

Ironically, I have been diagnosed with AIDS, still seen as a gay man's disease...I took a certain pleasure in informing the gender clinic that even though their program told me I could not live as a gay man, it looks like I'm going to die like one.

—Lou Sullivan,

an American activist and author known for being an early member of the GLBT Historical Society and for his advocacy as a proud trans man.

MINDFUL MOMENT

I accept myself exactly as I am now.

Understanding that both gender and sexual identity operate on a spectrum means that there's potential for your identity to continue to shift over time, as it likely has already. Embrace that evolution and embrace exactly where you are today on that journey.

I honestly didn't think that another opportunity would happen for me because of my transness. I was always beating myself up thinking that a trans woman of color would not be offered a [second] opportunity to be the centerfold in another television show. *Pose* was going to be the only opportunity.

—Michaela Jaé Rodriguez,
an American actor known for the show Pose, *which draws on the New York City ball scene of the 1980s.*

Something I've noticed particularly with the straight and cis people in my life is that they're so grateful when you choose an identity. There's an ease with being able to say, "Okay, you identify as this, and that's it. This is what I call you." But to make space for people to continue to transform or add things to their identities or take things away, actually feels more natural as opposed to choosing one thing and then sticking with it for the rest of your life. Especially for queer and trans people, because we are these constant investigators of ourselves and the world and our place in it.

—Bilal Baig,
a Canadian actor and writer known for co-creating the award-winning television series Sort Of.

I'VE NEVER BEEN A CRUSADER, BUT I'VE ALWAYS BEEN HONEST. I'VE NEVER BELIEVED IN LYING OR DENYING WHAT I AM TO ANYONE.

—Sylvester,

a singer-songwriter, queer trailblazer and beloved personality, who was often referred to as San Francisco's Queen of Disco.

We are told that we should not notice difference, but humans are tribal by nature. I've been followed in men's stores. I've gotten extra monitoring out of a concern that I might actually run off with things. I've struggled to get taxi cabs in major cities. The first thing people are going to notice is your skin color. Sexuality plays out differently. You have to choose to reveal that. Early in my career I was not so open about this out of a fear that that might disadvantage me.

—Raphael Bostic,

the 15th president of the Federal Reserve Bank of Atlanta. Bostic has been outspoken about the economic impacts of racism and more recently also came out publicly as gay.

There's no right or wrong way to be gay. No right or wrong way to come out. It's your journey, do it the way you wanna do it.

—Tan France,

a British-American fashion stylist and television personality who came to fame as the fashion expert on the Netflix show Queer Eye. *France, who is of Pakistani descent, is one of the first openly gay South Asian men to appear on a major TV series.*

As anyone who is gay will confirm, being "that way" is not something you become, it is a set of emotional and physical responses that just *are.*

—Lance Loud,

the first openly gay person to appear on American television. The 1973 documentary series, An American Family, *followed the Loud family in Santa Barbara, California. Lance's appearance on the show made him a gay icon.*

One of the most rewarding things [about playing this character] was that it really allowed me to work through my own defenses and my own walls that I put up.... It also allowed me to recognize all the moments in my past that I had created a story about what my mom said or what my dad said or what an ex-lover said to me, that at that time, I interpreted as a rejection, as a misunderstanding, as an emotional abandonment, when in reality, they were just doing their best to reach me but didn't know how.

—Lío Mehiel,
a Puerto Rican and Greek actor. Their performance in the film Mutt *(2023) earned them the U.S. Dramatic Special Jury Award at the Sundance Film Festival, making them the first transgender actor to receive the accolade.*

There's this other piece that I wrote about how we don't see two people of color, two Black queer people in media. There always has to be white gaze. What does that mean for us culturally to really never witness ourselves? I'm really invested in what it means when we unpack that loneliness. Because that's not the truth...there's still this humongous gap that just needs addressing for various reasons. I don't know if the mainstream media really wants to take on our whole truths.

—Kay Ulanday Barrett,
an American poet and writer. Their second book, More Than Organs *(2020), received a 2021 Stonewall Honor Book Award from the American Library Association and is a 2021 Lambda Literary Award Finalist. Barrett is an advocate for the trans, nonbinary and disabiltiy communities.*

MINDFUL MOMENT

What I feel right now is real.

Identities can change and shift, but wherever you are on the spectrum today, honor it! There's no time requirement for how long a feeling must be with you in order for it to be real—if you feel it today, it's real. You don't need to justify your feelings to yourself or anyone else.

What my mom eventually said to me was pretty much at the core of why I'm questioning comedy. She said to me, "The thing I regret is that I raised you as if you were straight. I didn't know any different. I'm so sorry. I knew well before you did, that your life was going to be so hard. I knew that, and I wanted, more than anything in the world, for that not to be the case. And now I know that I made it worse. I made it worse because I wanted you to change, because I knew that the world wouldn't."

—Hannah Gadsby,
an Australian comedian whose Netflix special Nanette *brought her an unexpected level of American fame.*

Being elected bishop is all the people in your local area wanting you to be a leader, and an installation service like this is all the other leaders also acknowledging that you're their colleague. It's really lovely to have that level of support, especially when you do something historic.

—Megan Rohrer,
an American bishop. They are the first transgender bishop in the Evangelical Lutheran Church, which also makes them the first trans bishop in any mainstream U.S. faith denomination.

Every person who comes to a queer self-understanding knows in one way or another that her stigmatization is connected with gender, the family, notions of individual freedom, the state, public speech, consumption and desire, nature and culture, maturation, reproductive politics, racial and national fantasy, class identity, truth and trust, censorship, intimate life and social display, terror and violence, health care, and deep cultural norms about the bearing of the body.

—Michael Warner,
from his book Fear of a Queer Planet *(1993). The book draws on the emerging queer politics of the early 1990s and shows how queer activists came to challenge basic assumptions about the social and political world.*

I have to go prove that we belong. I have to run a fast time to show that we're just as good and deserve to be acknowledged for what we're doing. But we shouldn't have to feel that. We should be able to just go out and run a fantastic race.

—J SOLLE,

an American athlete who finished third in the nonbinary category of the New York City Marathon in 2022. Nonbinary participation tripled in the race between 2021 and 2022.

Part of what constitutes the experience of minority is alienation from the minority identity that one supposedly has. So part of what makes you trans is not feeling trans—feeling like there are other trans people, maybe they're the real ones, and not being able to understand how it is to exist inside of being minoritized.

—Andrea Long Chu,
an American writer and book critic at New York Magazine.
Her book Females *(2019), an extended annotation of a lost play by Valerie Solanas, was a finalist for the Lambda Literary Award in Transgender Nonfiction.*

All that I seek I can find within me.

It's normal to want to share your experience with others while coming to a place of acceptance with your identity. Community is paramount to our overall health, but try not to forget that any answers you might be seeking, any approval you might be looking for, any acceptance you are trying to find—all of that lies within you.

It was a deliberate choice to make an album [like *Heartthrob*] that would gain access to the mainstream so that we could queer it a little bit. There really weren't that many people doing what we were doing. There were tons of them doing it in the underground, but no one was letting them up. We understand the privilege of the way we look and that we were twins, and that allowed us to be more mainstream than a lot of queer underground artists and we totally acknowledge that. But we had a job to do.

—Tegan Rain Quin,

a Canadian musician and one half of the twin musical duo Tegan and Sara. The indie pop group came to fame in the early 2000s and has released 10 studio albums in total.

What we do in bed, per se, as individuals, is nobody's business out there. But I'm saying, if we don't address humane human rights, we're gonna lose the ballgame.

—J.J. Belanger,

an American activist. A 1953 photo of him kissing Robert Block in a photo booth resurfaced in 2014 and spread widely on social media, even appearing in Time. *He was a member of the early gay rights group the Mattachine Society in Los Angeles.*

I think that LGBTQ folks have been just so visible, so courageous and so present that...it didn't feel like that this was the first time or the last time that this is going to happen. And I think that that difference that is really hard to articulate is what it feels like or is what it means when gay men have reached a certain level of of acceptance in the public sphere. I think we still haven't got there when it comes to trans and nonbinary folk. So I still think that we have still a larger conversation that us as gay men who have lots of power, access and privilege need to be at the forefront of continually centering that conversation.

—Wade Davis Jr.,
an activist and athlete. The former NFL player didn't come out publicly until 2012, nearly a decade after his football career had ended.

I was living with my mom, and one evening I didn't come home, and the next day she called from work and just said, "Is it a girl or a guy?" I said, "It's actually a guy," and she said, "Oh, cool, there's pasta in the fridge."

—Ivri Lider,

an Israeli pop singer who appeared on Out *magazine's "*Out *100" list in 2007.*

It took me so long to understand myself and my sexuality and that could be attributed in large part to the lack of images of women in relationships with each other. There's a bit more history of gay men depicted in romantic situations, but I'd seen so few examples when I was growing up of queer identity among women.

—Jenna Gribbon,
an American figurative painter whose work has been exhibited internationally. While her work focuses on the female form, it does so from a queer perspective.

As the parent of a gay child, and because of my work with gay people and their families since 1981, I know firsthand how homophobia and discrimination have affected our lives. We have all grown up with many myths and misconceptions about homosexuality and this creates innumerable problems in our society. We who have lifted the veil of ignorance, however, know that our gay and lesbian children are fine, responsible, contributing members of our communities. They deserve our love and support. They also deserve full human and civil rights and the respect accorded all citizens.

—Paulette Goodman,
from a letter she wrote to Barbara Bush in 1990. Goodman was the president of PFLAG (Parents, Family and Friends of Lesbians and Gays) from 1988 to 1992 and led the campaign to get PFLAG ads on D.C. Metrobuses.

The younger generations having these people to look up to and going, "OK, there's thriving gay men in this world," I think that's important because I never had that growing up and that's probably a part of why it took me so long. You can live your full life and not be fearful of anything. If I can play a small part in the younger generations and current players' lives to inspire them and not do what I did, then it is one of my life ambitions, complete.

—Zander Murray,
the first senior pro Scottish footballer to come out as gay.

Realizing that, although I've achieved success, there's been something missing in my life, and I've been searching for it but it's been there the whole time and it was me being completely, authentically me. And I didn't want to waste any more time.

—Eureka O'Hara,
an American drag queen and television personality. O'Hara rose to fame when she appeared on RuPaul's Drag Race *and later appeared on the show* We're Here, *in which she and several other* Drag Race *alums visit small-town America. She cites this experience as helping her realize she wanted to fully transition.*

MINDFUL MOMENT

One day and one step at a time.

While it's great to have a sense of those bigger benchmarks we'd like to hit, remember that we can only get there one day and one step at a time. Those steps might not feel like enough progress, but each one matters more than you know. Once you accept that good things take time, it'll be easier to keep moving toward those goals.

Resistance & Revolution

In order to build a better future, continue to amplify voices from both the past and present.

When I dare to be powerful, to use my strength in the service of my vision, then it becomes less and less important whether I am afraid.

—Audre Lorde,

from her book of essays and speeches, Sister Outsider *(1984). Lorde was a lesbian poet, writer, academic and civil rights activist whose works include* The First Cities *(1968),* Coal *(1976),* The Black Unicorn *(1978),* The Cancer Journals *(1980) and* A Burst of Light *(1988), which won the National Book Award in 1989.*

DARLING, I WANT MY GAY RIGHTS NOW!

—Marsha P. Johnson,

an outspoken advocate for gay rights. Johnson arrived in New York immediately after graduating high school with only $15 and a bag of clothes. At this time, she adopted the name Marsha P. Johnson; the "P" stood for "Pay it no mind," a phrase that became her motto. Johnson described herself as a gay person, a "transvestite" and a drag queen.

You must always be yourself no matter what the price. It is the highest form of morality.

—Candy Darling,

an American actress and transgender icon best known for her film work with Andy Warhol.

MINDFUL MOMENT

My strength and power are endless.

Remind yourself that these resources—your strength and your power—are infinite. It can be easy to think of them as finite, as if we have to be careful about using them so we don't deplete our stores, but shift your thinking to a mindset of abundance. Your mental stamina, your mental prowess, your emotional strength—these are all endless.

As the gay movement expands and becomes more assimilated, people who are not so easily assimilated will feel marginalized. Their marginalization creates another round of resistance. It's an inefficient and somewhat embarrassing process, but it's also extremely invigorating and democratic.

—JEFFREY ESCOFFIER,
an American author, activist and media strategist. His books include American Homo: Community and Perversity *(1998),* Bigger Than Life: The History of Gay Porn Cinema from Beefcake to Hardcore *(2009) and* Sex, Society, and the Making of Pornography *(2021).*

By aspiring to join the mainstream rather than continuing to figure out the ways we need to change it, we risk losing our gay and lesbian souls in order to gain the world.

—URVASHI VAID,
an Indian-born American LGBTQ+ activist, writer and lawyer renowned for her expertise in gender and sexuality law. She is the author of several books including Irresistible Revolution: Confronting Race, Class and the Assumptions of LGBT Politics *(2012), which critiqued the racial and gender bias of the mainstream LGBTQ+ movement.*

We want to see all gay people have a chance, equal rights, as straight people in America. We don't want to see gay people picked up on the streets for things like loitering or having sex or anything like that. S.T.A.R. [Street Transvestite Action Revolutionaries] originally was started by the president, Sylvia Lee Rivera, and Bubbles Rose Marie, and they asked me to come in as vice president. S.T.A.R. is a very revolutionary group. We believe in picking up the gun, starting a revolution if necessary. Our main goal is to see gay people liberated and free. We'd like to see our gay brothers and sisters out of jail and on the streets again.

—Marsha P. Johnson,

a popular figure in New York City's gay and art scene, including modeling for Andy Warhol and performing onstage with the drag performance troupe Hot Peaches. Johnson was known as the "mayor of Christopher Street" thanks to being a welcoming presence in the streets of Greenwich Village. The Martha P. Johnson State Park located in Brooklyn, New York, was named in her honor in 2020.

Reminder: Just four years ago I received death threats for adding black & brown stripes to the rainbow flag.
Don't let this month's glitter & sparkle erase the purpose of those stripes and the labor that got us here.
Queer history is now.

—Amber Hikes,
Chief Equity Officer at the ACLU. In 2017, Hikes introduced the world to the More Color, More Pride flag, which launched a global conversation around anti-racism in the LGBTQ+ community.

When I walk into the gym, I am treated no differently than any other man in all aspects of training—including the hard sparring that LA is known for. At a time of rising discrimination against transgender people in the United States, I am grateful to have received nothing but support and camaraderie from these boxers and their coaches, who have seen and respected me as the man I am.

—Patricio Manuel,
the first openly trans professional boxer in the U.S. and an Athlete Ally ambassador.

Abolishing unjust institutions is intergenerational work, and the work of a visible advocate is to inspire others, particularly young people to engage in radical, transformative work to create safe, loving spaces for LGBTQ+ community members.

—ANDREA ALEJANDRA GONZALES,
an American community organizer and educator. Gonzales made Teen Vogue*'s list of 21 under 21 Girls and Femmes Building a Better Future in 2020.*

We represent possibility. We represent choice, being able to create a life, a way of living, a way of loving, a way of looking that's outside of what we've been told that you should be.

—ALOK VAID-MENON,
on nonbinary and trans people. Vaid-Menon, who performs under the moniker ALOK, is an internationally acclaimed nonbinary author, poet, comedian and public speaker. They are the author of Femme in Public *(2017),* Beyond the Gender Binary *(2020) and* Your Wound / My Garden *(2021). Vaid-Menon is also the creator of #DeGenderFashion, a movement to degender the fashion and beauty industries.*

MINDFUL MOMENT

I take pride in who I am.

At first glance, this affirmation might not seem that revolutionary—isn't pride a form of self-love? Sure, but having pride in yourself, holding your head high, being exactly who you are—this is truly a revolutionary act. To be yourself, love yourself and take pride in yourself in a world that would rather you be a conformist just might actually be the most revolutionary thing you can do.

I want a dyke for president. I want a person with aids for president and I want a fag for vice president and I want someone with no health insurance and I want someone who grew up in a place where the earth is so saturated with toxic waste that they didn't have a choice about getting leukemia. I want a president that had an abortion at sixteen and I want a candidate who isn't the lesser of two evils and I want a president who lost their last lover to aids, who still sees that in their eyes every time they lay down to rest, who held their lover in their arms and knew they were dying. I want a president with no air conditioning, a president who has stood on line at the clinic, at the dmv, at the welfare office and has been unemployed and laid off and sexually harassed and gaybashed and deported. I want someone who has spent the night in the tombs and had a cross burned on their lawn and survived rape. I want someone who has been in love and been hurt, who respects sex, who has made mistakes and learned from them. I want a Black woman for president. I want someone with bad teeth ~~and an attitude~~, someone who has eaten ~~that nasty~~ hospital food, someone who crossdresses and has done drugs and been in therapy. I want someone who has committed civil disobedience. And I want to know why this isn't possible. I want to know why we started learning somewhere down the line that a president is always a clown: always a john and never a hooker. Always a boss and never a worker, always a liar, always a thief and never caught.

—Zoe Leonard,

from her piece "I want a president," which was written in 1992 in response to Eileen Myles's presidential bid. The piece was then widely recirculated during the 2016 U.S. election, serving as a call to action.

I AM NO LONGER ACCEPTING THE THINGS I CANNOT CHANGE. I AM CHANGING THE THINGS I CANNOT ACCEPT.

—Angela Davis,
an American political activist, philosopher, academic and author. Both a Marxist and a feminist, she was a longtime member of Communist Party USA and an active member of the Black Panther Party.

The point is, that as a Black gay man, I often ask, "From whom do I need protection?" And more often than not, the answer is, "I need to be protected from the police!"

—James Credle,
an LGBTQ+ and Vietnam Veterans activist who was also the former assistant dean of students at Rutgers University. Some of the LGBTQ+ organizations he's founded include the Newark Pride Alliance and Black and White Men Together.

MINDFUL MOMENT

I am stronger than anyone who attempts to suppress me.

We will come up against people who challenge us, people who don't understand us, people who feel threatened by us, people who are trying to suppress us because they sense all that we're capable of. Remember that you hold more strength than those people ever will—not necessarily in the physical sense but rather the fact that you possess high levels of compassion and empathy. Strength manifests in many ways.

It takes
no compromise to
give people their rights.
It takes
no money to
respect the individual.
It takes
no political deal to
give people freedom.
It takes
no survey to
remove repression.

—Harvey Milk,

a visionary human and civil rights leader who became one of the first openly gay elected officials in the U.S. when he won a seat on the San Francisco Board of Supervisors in 1977. His life, work and legacy have been celebrated ever since, including in the 2009 film Milk.

Queerness offers the promise of failure as a way of life... but it is up to us whether we choose to make good on that promise in a way that makes a detour around the usual markers of accomplishment and satisfaction.

—Jack Halberstam,

from his book, The Queer Art of Failure *(2011). Halberstam is a professor of English and comparative literature at the Institute for Research on Women, Gender, and Sexuality at Columbia University whose other books include* Female Masculinity (1998) and Gaga Feminism (2012).

YOU JUST HAVE TO DO WHAT YOU CAN AND DON'T GIVE UP. BECAUSE, SOMEDAY, THERE ARE GOING TO BE SURVIVORS.

—DANIEL SOTOMAYOR,

an American artist who became involved with AIDS activism after being diagnosed with HIV in 1987. He worked with the Chicago chapter of the AIDS Coalition to Unleash Power (ACT UP). Sotomayor was also the first openly gay and openly HIV-positive syndicated political cartoonist in the country. His editorial AIDS-centered cartoons covered such topics as politics, religion, public policy, the insurance industry, modern medicine, law enforcement, family dynamics, pop culture and the gay community itself.

When I founded the Gay Liberation Front in Los Angeles, being a longtime community organizer, I know that people have to have a measurable, chewable, doable, dramatic issue as a first order of business. It can't be ephemeral, it can't be victory in the future, it has to be right now.

—MORRIS KIGHT,

an American activist considered one of the original founding members of the gay and lesbian rights movement in the United States, cofounding the Los Angeles Gay and Lesbian Community Services Center in 1969.

There can be no justification,
no defense for social injustice.
The Constitution does not make exceptions.
We who have waited patiently to
be admitted to the vision of the Constitution
know the consequences of prejudice.

—MELVIN "MEL" BOOZER,
in his address to the Democratic National Convention (DNC) in New York City, August 1980. Boozer was a professor and activist for the African American, LGBTQ+ and HIV/AIDS communities.

Each generation of social justice activists and artists comes of age convinced that the battles they face are unique to history. History is a spiral of relapse and overlaps which push the envelope of identity and liberation a new step forward, then back, then further forward.

—JEANNE CÓRDOVA,
an American lesbian and gay rights activist. She was a founder of the newspaper The Lesbian Tide, *which was a pivotal part of early gay rights activism on the West Coast.*

MINDFUL MOMENT

I am not confused about who I am as a queer person.

We live in a society where, unfortunately, heterosexuality is the dominant culture, and for queer folks, it can be easy to feel confused about our place. Here's your reminder to resist fitting in. Be proud of who you are, even if who you are doesn't match this heteronormative narrative. Resist being anything you're not.

We were sick and tired of being criminalized, pathologized, demonized, of being made to hide who we were and having our rights to live as human beings denied.

—Mark Gillespie,

an Australian activist who was present at the 1978 march by the Gay Solidarity Group in Sydney, Australia. The march began as a celebratory event—with the group having secured a permit—but ended in unprecedented police brutality. It is credited as helping to galvanize the queer Australian community into political action.

Yes, we must negotiate.
Yes, we must lobby.
Yes, we must litigate.
But we must also remember where we come from, and return to allowing that rage to be expressed and not think for a minute that there is something not respectable about that.

—Virginia Apuzzo,

an American gay rights and AIDS activist who is also the former executive director of the National Lesbian and Gay Task Force.

True community is based upon equality, mutuality, and reciprocity. It affirms the richness of individual diversity as well as the common human ties that bind us together.

—Pauli Murray,

an American civil rights activist, poet, writer and labor organizer. She was one of the first women—and the first African American woman—to be ordained as an Episcopal priest.

I deserve to feel safe.

The truth is that in the real world, safety won't always be a guarantee. Violence against queer people is a terrifying reality, but that doesn't mean you don't deserve to feel safe. This affirmation is a reminder of this basic right everyone is entitled to. Use this to guide you through your acts of resistance as a queer person. Simply knowing you deserve to feel safe each day will hopefully make that a more plausible reality.

That's the thing about history, you know, history is capital. The reason why I think the distinctions are worth knowing about is while communal responses, political responses, like ACT UP are incredibly valuable and noteworthy, there's also power in the individual voice. It was six gay men, who had no idea that they were surrounded by a community that was going to come into formation, who made this [SILENCE = DEATH] poster. And I think for an activist in 2050, after I'm gone, and you're old, it would be helpful to know that a room full of people can seize the commons. You don't need to fully organize a movement in order to utilize the commons.

—Avram Finkelstein,
an American writer and gay rights activist.
Finkelstein is a member of the AIDS art collective Gran Fury.

Some of them say that we're sick, or crazy, and some of them think that we're the most gorgeous, special things on Earth.

—Venus Xtravaganza,
an American transgender performer best known for her appearance in the 1990 documentary film Paris is Burning.

NO GOVERNMENT HAS THE RIGHT TO TELL ITS CITIZENS WHEN OR WHOM TO LOVE.

—Rita Mae Brown,

an American feminist writer best known for her coming-of-age autobiographical novel, Rubyfruit Jungle. *Brown was active in a number of civil rights campaigns and criticized the marginalization of lesbians within feminist groups. She received the Pioneer Award for lifetime achievement at the Lambda Literary Awards in 2015.*

The [queer] community press [has been], really, the only resource other than word of mouth for letting people know that a new world, a new outlook, and a new community [are] in formation.

—John D'Emilio,

an American writer and retired professor whose work and research focused on gay and lesbian studies as well as social movements. He's the author of such books as Sexual Politics, Sexual Communities: The Making of a Homosexual Minority in the United States *(1983),* The World Turned: Essays on Gay History, Politics, and Culture *(2002) and* The Prophet: The Life and Times of Bayard Rustin *(2003).*

I feel as though it is my duty to be a part of solutions to hatred rather than the cause of it. I remember the feeling of hopelessness as I dealt with homophobia and transphobia throughout my youth, and I plan on being a part of the generation that puts a cap to it. Everyone deserves to be free and use their voice to express themselves.

—Nico Craig,
an American music producer and activist. He was named a 2021 Human Rights Campaign ambassador for their activism efforts at their high school in Culver City, California.

One of the lessons I have learned in trying to live with history is that for every repression, we have found a suitable form of resistance. Our history is the chronicle of our vitality, our passion, our cunning, and at many times, our integrity.

—Joan Nestle,
an American writer, editor and the founder of the Lesbian Herstory Archives.

I deserve to feel peace.

We might be fighting battles out in the world as queer folks—for our rights, for equality—and those battles might involve a lot of strife and turmoil. But that doesn't mean our personal lives can't also have a sense of peace. It's actually necessary if we are going to continue to be part of the revolution—we have to find inner peace so we can bring that energy to the revolution.

Everybody wants to leave something behind them, some impression, some mark upon the world. Then you think, you've left a mark on the world if you just get through it and a few people remember your name. You don't have to bend the whole world...it's better to just enjoy it, pay your dues and enjoy it. If you shoot an arrow and it goes real high, hooray for you.

—Dorian Corey,
an American drag performer and fashion designer who appeared in the documentary Paris is Burning *(1990).*

WE NEED, IN EVERY COMMUNITY, A GROUP OF ANGELIC TROUBLEMAKERS.

—Bayard Rustin,
an American activist for civil rights, nonviolence, socialism and gay rights.

All my life, I have maintained that the people of the world can learn to live together in peace if they are not brought up in prejudice.

—Josephine Baker,

an American dancer who made her career in Paris in the 1920s. A prolific activist throughout World War II and the American civil rights movement, Baker adopted 12 children from different countries and dubbed her family "the rainbow tribe."

I'm not missing a minute of this— it's the revolution!

—Sylvia Rivera,

an American trans activist. A legendary figure and integral force at the 1969 Stonewall Inn uprising, her activism was heavily focused on making trans people of color a part of larger gay rights movements. She was a close friend of Marsha P. Johnson, with whom she started the Street Transvestite Action Revolutionaries (STAR) around 1971. The group became a space to organize and discuss issues facing the transgender community in New York City and they also had a building, STAR House, that provided lodging for those in need.

I feel they should let [us] do
what we want to.
To each his own.
There are a lot of
homosexuals in Florida.
This is the life we want to live.
I'm satisfied with this life
and I'm not going to change it.

—JANNETTE LOUISE SPIRES,
an American activist. Spires is known for an instance in 1970 in which she and her partner, Thelma Jean Harris, were denied a marriage license by the state of Florida, despite there being no laws against it at the time.

**We must realize that as we expect to
be persecuted, so shall we be persecuted.
As we prepare for war, even though
we call it defense, we bring war ever closer.
As we listen to the voice of doom,
so shall we be doomed.
What wevproject shall come to pass.
When the individual begins to reevaluate himself
and his thoughts, when he sees that his thoughts and
actions are reflected by the leaders he elects,
that what his country projects in the community of
nations are what he himself has accepted,
then perhaps there can be peace on earth.**

—DEL MARTIN,
a lesbian rights activist whose work began in the 1950s when she cofounded the first lesbian rights organization, the Daughters of Bilitis. She and her partner Phyllis Ann Lyon were also the first lesbian couple to join the National Organization for Women.

MINDFUL MOMENT

My boundaries are being respected.

When people don't understand you, questions might follow, but remember to have your boundaries respected—physically and emotionally. Whether someone encroaches on your personal space, pries too deeply into your life or expects you to help them gain a better understanding of queer folks, you can always enact a boundary when it's needed.

They think that when they pick on us that they're picking on the weakest. Well, they made a mistake this time! We're going to show them just how strong we are. They can't get away with this shit anymore! No more shit!

—Chris Bearchell,

a Canadian activist. She was a founding or early member of some of the first queer organizations in Canada, including GATE (the Gay Alliance Towards Equality), the Lesbian Organization of Toronto and the Coalition for Lesbian and Gay Rights in Ontario.

It's got to stop somewhere, and it won't unless somebody steps forward and takes a stand. I guess that's me.

—Sir Lady Java,

an American transgender rights activist, exotic dancer, singer, comedian and actress. She was active in television, radio and film from the mid-1960s to 1970s.

The preference for [the term] "queer" represents, among other things, an aggressive impulse of generalizations; it rejects a minoritizing logic of toleration or simple political interest-representation in favor of a more thorough resistance to regimes of the normal.... For both academics and activists, "queer" gets a critical edge by defining itself against the normal rather than the heterosexual.

—MICHAEL WARNER,

from his book Fear of a Queer Planet *(1993), which explores queerness, postmodernism and shifts in the cultural politics surrounding sexuality.*

Every gay and lesbian person who has been lucky enough to survive the turmoil of growing up is a survivor. Survivors always have an obligation to those who will face the same challenges.

—BOB PARIS,

a former American professional bodybuilder. When he came out publicly in 1989, Paris became the first openly gay professional athlete to still be an active competitor.

I still hear people say that I should not be talking about the rights of lesbian and gay people and I should stick to the issue of racial justice. But I hasten to remind them that Martin Luther King Jr. said, "Injustice anywhere is a threat to justice everywhere."

—Coretta Scott King,

activist and wife of Dr. Martin Luther King Jr. Her activism with regard to racial inequality dates back all the way to her teens, though it was in 1983, on the 20th anniversary of her husband's March on Washington, that she pledged her support for the Gay and Civil Rights Act that was before Congress at the time.

MINDFUL MOMENT

This body makes things happen.

Be rooted in your physical self—this is where all your acts of resistance originate. Remind yourself how much you are actually doing on a daily basis, how much you have already done, how much you have yet to do. You are a vessel for change, and you have made so many things happen already.

We struggle and fight for our joy — an unreserved and unapologetic joy that springs from our ability to live as we are. It's a joy worth fighting for and it's this joy that links all of our struggles together.

—Lady Phyll,

a British political activist, cofounder of UK Black Pride and the Executive Director of Kaleidoscope Trust, an organization that campaigns for the human rights of LGBTQ+ people worldwide.

Family belongs to community, and community takes its cues from family. We need to go back to real community engagement that sees us as people. We need to take back our lives by engaging our families and educating our communities.

—Beverley Ditsie,

a South African artist, lesbian activist and filmmaker. She was a founding member of both the Gay and Lesbian Organisation of Witwatersrand and the first Pride March in South Africa.

I had to fight for the rights I didn't have because no one was fighting for them fully for me.... If you see a problem, you're never too small of a person to make a change and to speak out about that problem.

—Ose Arheghan,

an American activist. They were chosen as the 2017 Student Advocate of the Year by GLSEN, a leading education organization creating safe and inclusive K-12 education for LGBTQ+ youth.

Not everyone is equipped for activism in the traditional sense—marching, writing letters to officials—but dedicating your life to understanding yourself can be its own form of protest, especially when the world tells you that you don't exist.

—Samra Habib,

from their bestselling book, We Have Always Been Here: A Queer Muslim Memoir *(2019). Habib is also well known for the photography project Just Me and Allah, which they launched in 2014 to document the lives of LGBTQ+ Muslims.*

I once worried that there was no place for trans people like me to participate in any way in our politics. Since coming out, though, I've seen that change is possible and I've learned that the only things that are truly impossible are the things we don't try. You can run, you can win and you can serve.

—Sarah McBride,

an American senator and activist. On November 3, 2020, she became the first openly transgender person elected to a state senate in the U.S. when she won a seat in the Delaware Senate.

They can't ever say now that a gay man can't play in the majors, because I'm a gay man and I made it.

—Glenn Burke,
a professional baseball player for the LA Dodgers and the Oakland A's from 1976 to 1979.

MINDFUL MOMENT

I am a force the world needs.

Without your voice, without your presence, without your acts of resistance, the world would be very different. The world needs you every single day. Every contribution you make matters more than you know, and each one is part of a collective queer resistance that is absolutely necessary. The world needs you.

BOOK BANS AREN'T JUST BOOK BANS.... THEY'RE ATTEMPTS TO ERASE PEOPLE LIKE ME, TO SCARE US BACK INTO INVISIBILITY AND IRRELEVANCE. WE WILL BE NEITHER.

—JACK PETOCZ,
an American activist and strategist at Gen-Z for Change.

This outbreak of Gay Pride triggered a reaction felt around the world. When you hear, "Remember Stonewall," you should all remember that it was because of police brutality against our community that Stonewall is celebrated today, tomorrow, and will be forever!

—JAMES CREDLE,
an American academic administrator, counselor and Vietnam Veterans and LGBTQ+ rights activist. Credle is the former assistant dean of students at Rutgers University, and he founded a number of LGBTQ+ organizations, including the Newark Pride Alliance and Black and White Men Together.

No pride for some of us without liberation for all of us.

—Marsha P. Johnson,

a trans activist who was on the front lines of the Stonewall Riots on June 28, 1969—an experience that helped to galvanize the gay rights movement. Following the raid that night, Johnson and her good friend Sylvia Rivera led a series of protests throughout the city. Throughout the 1970s, Johnson's visibility within the gay rights movement only increased.

I protested shoulder to shoulder with my lesbian, gay, bisexual, and transgender [siblings] for the right to be validated and treated like a person. I wasn't a second-class citizen then and won't be treated like one now!

—Yvonne Ritter,
an American trans and AIDS activist who was present at the Stonewall Riots. She went on to become a nurse working with HIV patients and also helped counsel trans folks at the LGBT Community Center in New York.

WHEN HOPE IS GONE, FIGHT LIKE SYLVIA! FIERCELY 'TIL THE VERY END

—Rusty Mae Moore,
an American trans activist and educator. She and prolific activist Sylvia Rivera ran the homeless shelter Transy House, which served the homeless trans community, throughout the 1990s and 2000s.

Listening to Harvey Milk's recording gave me my life because for the very first time I heard a leader leading with hope not fear and that vision of hope included me. I didn't know it was possible to be out of the closet or to lead with anything other than fear. It gave me the hope to start living my life.

—Dustin Lance Black,
a screenwriter and activist who wrote the film Milk, *which won him the Academy Award for Best Original Screenplay in 2009.*

I PROMISED MYSELF NEVER TO STOP DOWN TO MY LAST BREATH.

—Pedro Zamora,
a Cuban-American HIV/AIDS educator and former cast member on The Real World: San Francisco. *When he appeared on the show in 1994, he was one of the first openly gay men to appear regularly on U.S. television. He helped humanize those living with HIV/AIDS during some of the deadliest years of the epidemic.*

Equality means more than passing laws. The struggle is really won in the hearts and minds of the community, where it really counts.

—Barbara Gittings,

an American LGBTQ+ rights activist. She organized the New York chapter of the Daughters of Bilitis, a lesbian organization, from 1958 to 1963.

I am an Asian American woman, a mother, and a lesbian. Because these things are difficult to put into a neat package, because I am genuinely different, I know that I live in the face of this country's determination to destroy me, to negate me, to render me invisible.... I have a three-year-old daughter and any risk I must take to build a free future for myself and my daughter is worth it. It is as concrete and as abstract as that.

—Michiyo Cornell,
a Japanese-American poet and activist whose work focused on the lesbian and Asian American communities.

MINDFUL MOMENT

I am resilient in the face of challenges.

Being part of a queer revolution requires a limitless supply of resilience. You are going to experience many hardships, but they won't get you down, they won't defeat you—showing up to do the work knowing it won't be easy is true resilience. Tap into those resilience reserves every single day.

As long as the Earth can make
a spring every year, I can.
As long as the Earth can flower and
produce nurturing fruit,
I can, because I'm the Earth.
I won't give up until the Earth gives up.

—ALICE WALKER,
an American novelist, short story writer, poet and social activist. Her novel The Color Purple *won the Pulitzer Prize for Fiction in 1983, making her the first African-American woman to win the prestigious accolade.*

Being unapologetically me is a statement in itself. It's a parade in itself. Just me being gay every day is already a political statement, let's just say that. And so moving forward, the best that I can do is just continue what I have been doing: standing up for everything I believe in and really speaking up for my gay brothers and sisters, especially my trans brothers and sisters, which is what the world really can't grasp on right now.

—BRETMAN ROCK,
a Filipino beauty influencer and social media personality. He came to fame through his YouTube channel and now boasts a following of more than 18 million on Instagram.

We do not have the responsibility of making gay life look good to straights so that they will accept us. I am not at all interested in promoting a cleaned up image to a straight world which is twice as corrupt and ten times as sick.

—Vito Russo,

an American LGBTQ+ activist, film historian and author. His 1981 book, The Celluloid Closet, *was described in* The New York Times *as "an essential reference book" on homosexuality in the U.S. film industry.*

MINDFUL MOMENT

I am aligned with my purpose.

You are exactly what the resistance needs. Your queer, authentic life matters matters so deeply. That is your purpose. The issues facing the wider queer community are huge, and we can't take on everything. Use this affirmation as a reminder that wherever you find yourself in the community, whatever cause you find yourself fighting for, you are doing as much as you can and you are aligned with your purpose. It matters and it's revolutionary.

This is the gay community, not some heterosexual suburb where everyone has to be just like everyone else.

—Dick Leitsch,

an American activist best known for leading a Sip-In in 1966 in which a group of activists challenged a New York regulation effectively prohibiting bars from serving queer people.

Marriage is a magic word. And it is magic throughout the world. It has to do with our dignity as human beings, to be who we are openly.

—Edie Windsor,

a queer rights activist who made a huge impact on the fight for marriage equality. Windsor was the lead plaintiff in a Supreme Court case that led to a landmark decision in 2013, when the Supreme Court ruled that Section 3 of the Defense of Marriage Act (DOMA) is unconstitutional and that the federal government can't discriminate against married lesbian and gay couples for the purposes of determining federal benefits and protections.

I always imagined I would have a life very different from the one that was imagined for me, but I understood from a very early time that I would have to revolt in order to make that life. Now I am convinced that in any creativity there exists this element of revolt.

—Leonor Fini,
a bisexual Italian surrealist painter, designer, illustrator and author.

Pride works in direct opposition to internalized oppression. The latter provides a fertile ground for shame, denial, self-hatred, and fear. The former encourages anger, strength, and joy. To transform self-hatred into pride is a fundamental act of resistance.

—Eli Clare,
from his book, Exile and Pride: Disability, Queerness, and Liberation *(1999), which details his experiences as a white disabled genderqueer activist and writer.*

My point is that when the right wing draws us into these ontological battles over the meaning of sex, they're not doing it from any kind of good faith position. And yet we keep bringing out experts. I just feel like it's the wrong terrain for that. We need to be focusing on the harm that people face—like these kids in Alabama who suddenly have their transition-related medical care taken away—instead of talking about what gender is and where it comes from.

—PAISLEY CURRAH,

a professor, writer and political scientist. His work for the trans rights movement includes his book, Sex Is as Sex Does: Governing Transgender Identity *(2022), which examines the politics of sex classification in the United States.*

WE'RE DYING IN THIS STATE. WHAT ARE YOU GOING TO DO ABOUT AIDS?

—BOB RAFSKY,

in a 1992 confrontation with then-governor Bill Clinton, who was just beginning his campaign for president. During the fundraiser, the American writer, publicist and HIV/AIDS activist began a line of questioning as to how Clinton would handle the AIDS epidemic. Unsatisfied with the answers he got, Rafsky continued to press Clinton, eventually getting him to commit to fight AIDS—the first mainstream presidential candidate to do so.

The time has come for us to walk in the sunshine. We don't have to ask permission to do it. Here we are!

—Martha Shelley,

an American writer, activist and poet. She was a writer for the Gay Liberation Front's newsletter Come Out! *Her books include* Lovers and Mothers *(1981),* The Throne in the Heart of the Sea *(2011) and* A Meteor Shower *(2019).*

YOUR SILENCE WILL NOT PROTECT YOU.

—Audre Lorde,
an American writer, author, academic and activist. In her writing, she frequently expressed her anger at the treatment of people of color, women and LGBTQ+ folk. To many in the queer community, staying silent and in the closet felt like a safety blanket. However, Lorde encouraged them to step out into the light, telling them that the only true safety is in making yourself known and demanding the acceptance and respect that is your right.

Freedom from hate, unconditionally; Freedom from self-pity (even through all the pain and bad news); Freedom from fear of possibly doing something that might possibly help another more than it might himself; and Freedom from the kind of pride that might make a man think that he was better than his brother or his neighbor.

—Duke Ellington,
from his autobiography Music Is My Mistress, *in which he lists the above as jazz composer Billy Strayhorn's "Four Major Moral Freedoms." Strayhorn, who was openly gay, collaborated with Ellington on numerous works including* Such Sweet Thunder *and* The Nutcracker Suite.

MINDFUL MOMENT

My existence is revolutionary.

Resistance and revolution can be as large as a city-wide protest or a Pride March in June, but resistance and revolution can also be as small as showing up every day as your most authentic, queer self. Coming as you are is itself an act of resistance—you are challenging the cultural norms simply because you exist as physical proof that there are other experiences. Your existence truly is revolutionary.

Whether the unsympathetic majority approves or not, it looks as though the third sex is here to stay.

—Edythe Eyde,

an American activist. She founded the lesbian publication Vice Versa, *which, although it only lasted nine issues, helped set the agenda for future mainstream gay publications.*

You have to act as if it were possible to radically transform the world. And you have to do it all the time.

—Angela Davis,

an American political activist, philosopher, academic and author. Her extensive publishing history includes the books If They Come in the Morning: Voices of Resistance *(1971),* Angela Davis: An Autobiography *(1974),* Women, Race and Class *(1981),* Are Prisons Obsolete *(2003),* Abolition Democracy: Beyond Empire, Prisons, and Torture *(2005) and* Abolition. Feminism. Now. *(2022).*

THE SUREST WAY TO GET A BUNCH OF QUEERS TO DO ANYTHING IS TO MAKE A RULE NONSENSICALLY FORBIDDING US FROM DOING IT.

—Zena Sharman,

from her book The Remedy: Queer and Trans Voices on Health and Health Care, *which won the Lambda Literary Award for Best Anthology in 2017.*

I'm running through the tape but this baton has been passed from generation to generation of #LGBTQ activists in Michigan. And we are telling future generations that they now have a future.

—Jeremy Moss,

a Michigan Senator who sponsored a historic 2023 bill that expanded the Elliott-Larsen Civil Rights Act—which prohibits discrimination based on religion, race, sex and other protected classes—to include LGBTQ+ protections.

WE OWE THIS CULTURE NOTHING BUT OUR DETERMINATION TO REPLACE IT.

—Allen Young,

an American journalist, author and writer. Some of his books and anthologies include After You're Out: Personal Experiences of Gay Men and Lesbian Women *(1975),* Out of the Closets: Voices of Gay Liberation *(1992) and his autobiography,* Left, Gay & Green: A Writer's Life *(2018).*

We came battle-scarred and angry to topple your racist, sexist, hateful society. In one fell swoop, we came to destroy by our mere presence your labels and stereotypes with which you've oppressed us for centuries. And we came with love and open hearts to challenge your hate and secrecy.

—Kiyoshi Kuromiya,

a Japanese-American author and civil rights, anti-war, gay liberation and HIV/AIDS activist who was present for the first Gay Pride Parade in 1970.

MINDFUL MOMENT

I can say no whenever I need to.

This is a big one, but sometimes the most obvious things are the ones we most easily forget. When working to be part of a revolution, your impulse might be to take on all of the issues at once (there are so many of them, and they all matter). But saying no when you need to will prevent you from depleting yourself, which is the only way the revolution can move forward.

I believe that telling our stories, first to ourselves and then to one another and the world, is a revolutionary act.

—JANET MOCK,

a transgender rights activist, author and TV host. Her work as a writer, director and producer on the show Pose *earned her Emmy nominations in 2019 and 2021.*

I feel now that I can begin to put our lives in a larger framework. Ma, a larger framework! The outlines for us are time and blood, but today there is breadth possible through making connections with others involved in community struggle.
In loving ourselves for who we are—American women of color—we can make a vision for the future where we are free to fulfill our human potential.
This new framework will not support repression, hatred, exploitation and isolation, but will be a human and beautiful framework, created in a community, bonded not by color, sex or class, but by love and the common goal for the liberation of mind, heart and spirit.

—MERLE WOO,

from her biographical essay "Letter to Ma." Woo is an Asian American poet, academic and activist. "Letter to Ma" deals with her mother's silence surrounding her lesbian lifestyle.

Acknowledgments

This book is indebted to the work of all of the incredible activists, authors, musicians, writers, artists and everyday people contained within who paved the way for generations to come. Their work will not be forgotten and this book serves to honor them.

This book is also indebted to the extensive research undertaken by Matthew Riemer and Leighton Brown, who wrote the seminal book *We Are Everywhere: Protest, Power, and Pride in the History of Queer Liberation*. The wonderful podcast and oral history archive *Making Gay History* was also a wonderful source of information.

—J. Katherine

About the Authors

J. Katherine's essays have appeared in *Hotel Amerika*, *Quarter After Eight*, *saltfront* and *After Happy Hour Review*, among others. She is currently based in Detroit and holds an MFA in creative writing from Northern Michigan University.

Jim Obergefell is a speaker on LGBTQ+ equality and civil rights and cofounder of Equality Vines, the first cause-based wine label to support organizations dedicated to equality. He is the named plaintiff in Obergefell v. Hodges, the landmark U.S. Supreme Court decision that affirmed the fundamental right to marry for same sex couples.

Jim is president of the WebQ Board of Directors and sits on advisory boards for the GLBT Historical Society and the Mattachine Society of Washington, D.C. He is a former SAGE board member, former Family Equality staff member and coauthor of the book *Love Wins*, published by William Morrow.

LGBTQ Nation is the country's most popular LGBTQ+ news site, reporting on issues relevant to the lesbian, gay, bisexual, transgender and queer community.

Media Lab Books
For inquiries, call 646-449-8614

Published by Topix Media Lab
14 Wall Street, Suite 3C
New York, NY 10005

Printed in Korea

ISBN-13: 978-1-956403-47-3
ISBN-10: 1-956403-47-7

PA-F23-1

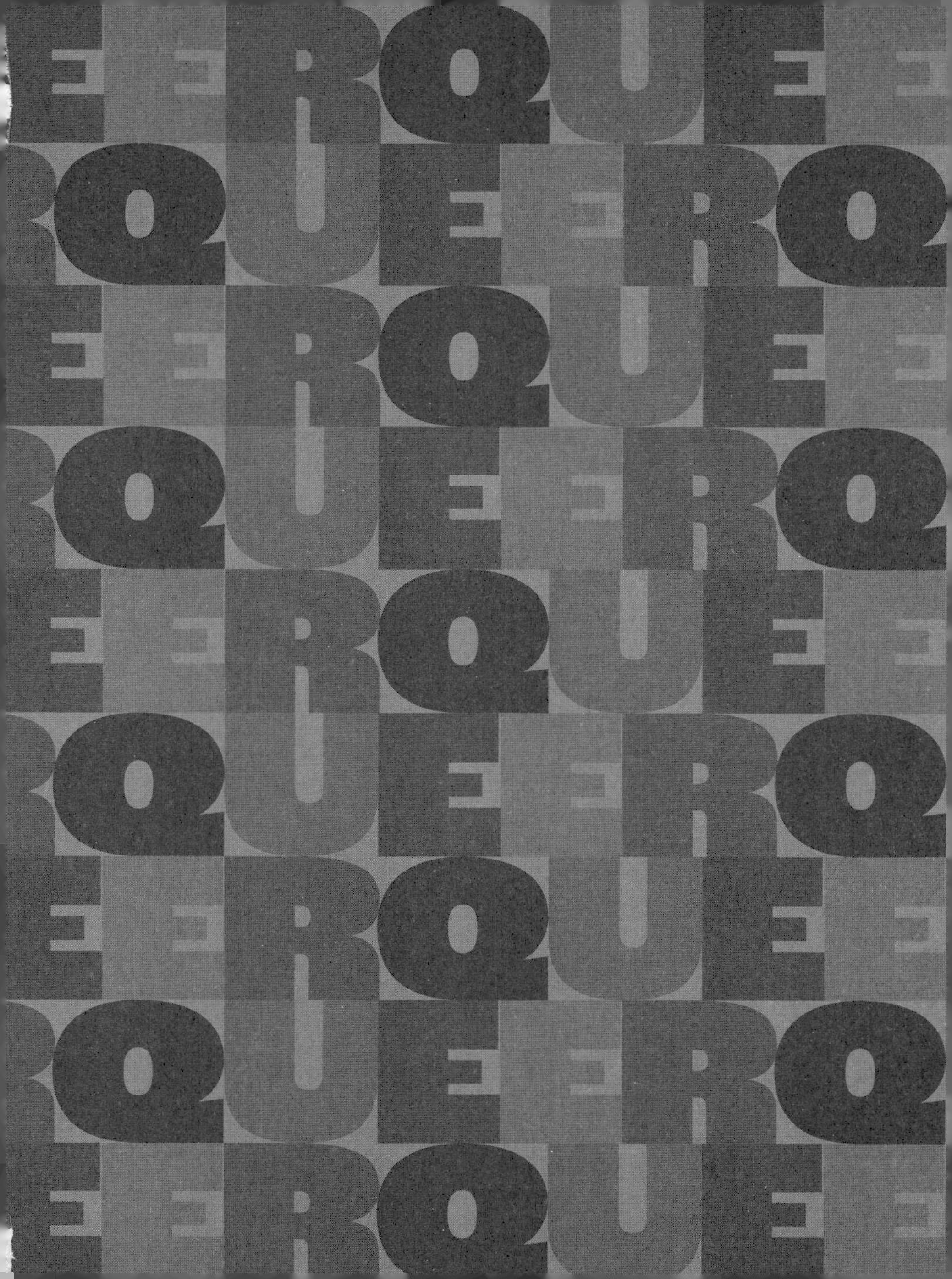

D0315352

ALL OF ME

ALTO SAX

Words and Music by SEYMOUR SIMONS
and GERALD MARKS

ALL THE THINGS YOU ARE

APRIL IN PARIS

ALTO SAX

Words by E.Y. "YIP" HARBURG
Music by VERNON DUKE

AUTUMN IN NEW YORK

AUTUMN LEAVES

English Lyric by JOHNNY MERCER
French Lyric by JACQUES PREVERT
Music by JOSEPH KOSMA

BEWITCHED

ALTO SAX

Words by LORENZ HART
Music by RICHARD RODGERS

BEYOND THE SEA

Lyrics by JACK LAWRENCE
Music by CHARLES TRENET and ALBERT LASRY
Original French Lyric to "La Mer" by CHARLES TRENET

ALTO SAX

THE BLUE ROOM

ALTO SAX

Words by LORENZ HART
Music by RICHARD RODGERS

BLUE SKIES

ALTO SAX

Words and Music by
IRVING BERLIN

BLUESETTE

ALTO SAX

Words by NORMAN GIMBEL
Music by JEAN THIELEMANS

BODY AND SOUL

ALTO SAX

Words by EDWARD HEYMAN,
ROBERT SOUR and FRANK EYTON
Music by JOHN GREEN

BUT BEAUTIFUL

ALTO SAX

Words by JOHNNY BURKE
Music by JIMMY VAN HEUSEN

CAN'T HELP LOVIN' DAT MAN

ALTO SAX

Lyrics by OSCAR HAMMERSTEIN II
Music by JEROME KERN

CARAVAN

ALTO SAX

Words and Music by DUKE ELLINGTON,
IRVING MILLS and JUAN TIZOL

CHARADE

ALTO SAX

By HENRY MANCINI

CHEEK TO CHEEK

ALTO SAX

Words and Music by
IRVING BERLIN

COME RAIN OR COME SHINE

ALTO SAX

Words by JOHNNY MERCER
Music by HAROLD ARLEN

DANCING ON THE CEILING

ALTO SAX

Words by LORENZ HART
Music by RICHARD RODGERS

DEARLY BELOVED

ALTO SAX

Music by JEROME KERN
Words by JOHNNY MERCER

DO NOTHIN' TILL YOU HEAR FROM ME

ALTO SAX

Words and Music by DUKE ELLINGTON
and BOB RUSSELL

Moderate Swing

DON'T GET AROUND MUCH ANYMORE

DREAMSVILLE

ALTO SAX

By HENRY MANCINI

Slowly

Gmaj9 Dm7 Gmaj9 Dm7 C♯9

Gm9/C C9 Am7 B♭m7 Bm7 E7 Am7 D7♭9

Gmaj9 Dm7 Gmaj9 Dm7 C♯9

Gm9/C C9 Am7 B♭m7 Am9 G♯9♯11 Gmaj9

C♯m7♭5 F♯7♭9 Bm9 E7♭9 C♯m7 A C9

D♯m7♭5 G♯9 C♯m7♭5 F♯7♭9 Bm7♭5 E7 Am7 D7♭9

Gmaj9 Dm7 Gmaj9 Dm7 C♯9

Gm9/C C9 Am7 B♭m7 Am9 G♯9♯11 1. Gmaj9 2. Gmaj9

FALLING IN LOVE WITH LOVE

ALTO SAX

Words by LORENZ HART
Music by RICHARD RODGERS

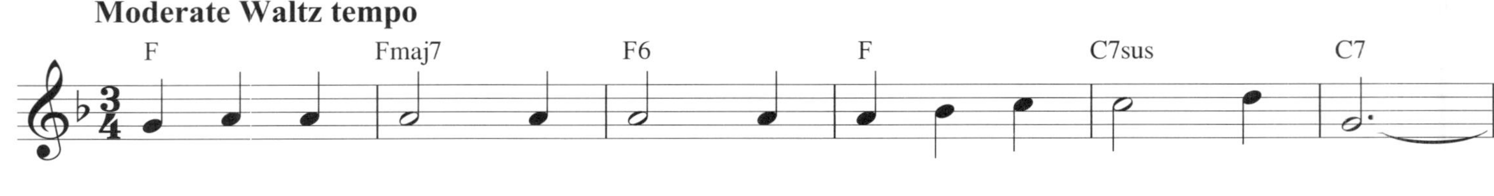

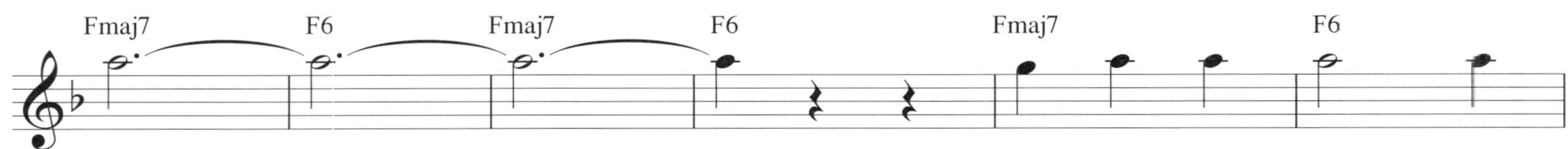

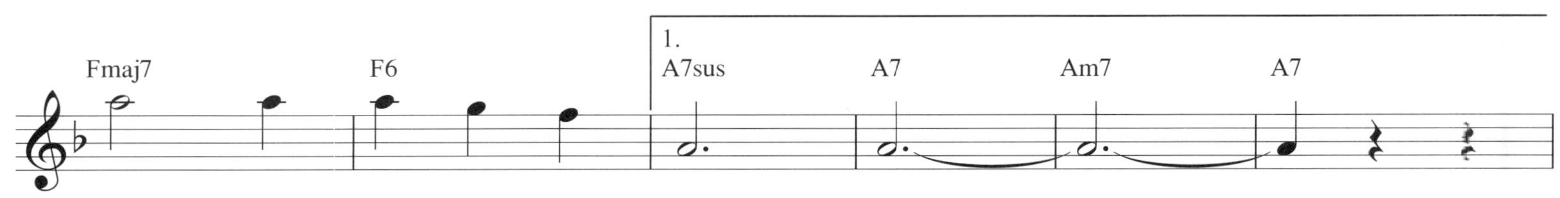

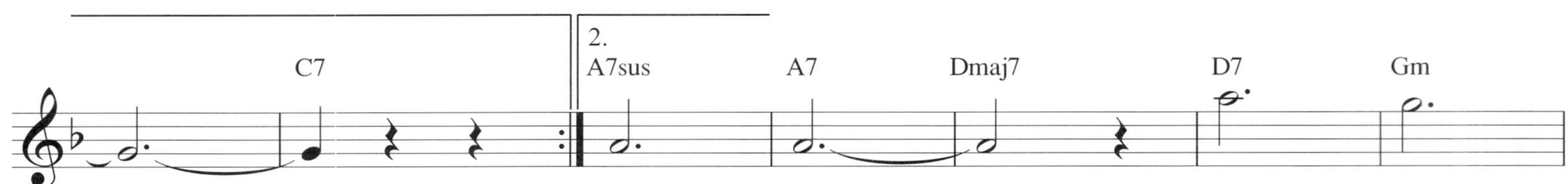

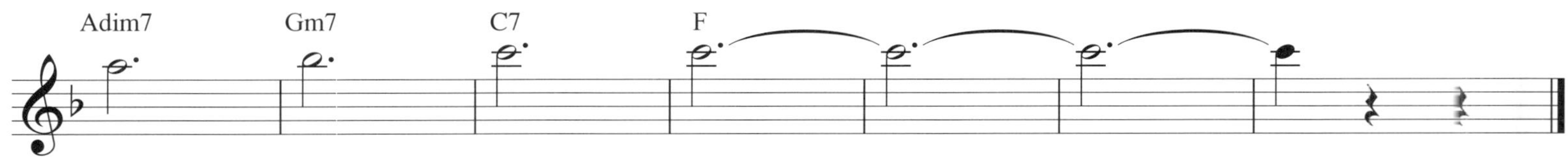

A FINE ROMANCE

ALTO SAX

Words by DOROTHY FIELDS
Music by JEROME KERN

Moderately

G D7 D7♯5

G D7 G

E13 E♭13 D13 Am7 D7 G6 Bm7

E7 C♯13 C13 B7 Cmaj7 C♯7♯5 D7 G

G♯dim7 D7 D7♯5 G

D11 D9 G6 G7 E7

Am7 E7 C A7♭9 G D7

1. G 2. G6

FLY ME TO THE MOON
(In Other Words)

ALTO SAX

Words and Music by
BART HOWARD

GEORGIA ON MY MIND

ALTO SAX

Words by STUART GORRELL
Music by HOAGY CARMICHAEL

Slowly

C E7 Am Am/G D/F♯ Fm6

Em7 A7 Dm7 G7 Em7 A7♭9 Dm7 G7♯5

C E7 Am Am/G D/F♯ Fm6

Em7 A7 Dm7 D9 G13 C B♭9 C E7 Am Dm6

Am F7 Am Dm6 Am7 D7 Am G♯dim7

C6/G F♯m7♭5 B7 Em7 C♯dim7 Dm7 G7 C

E7 Am Am/G D/F♯ Fm6 Em7 A7

Dm7 D9 G13 1. C Am7 Dm7 G7 G7♯5 2. C G7♯5 C6

HERE'S THAT RAINY DAY

ALTO SAX

Words by JOHNNY BURKE
Music by JIMMY VAN HEUSEN

HERE'S TO LIFE

ALTO SAX

Music by ARTIE BUTLER
Lyrics by PHYLLIS MOLINARY

HONEYSUCKLE ROSE

ALTO SAX

Words by ANDY RAZAF
Music by THOMAS "FATS" WALLER

HOW DEEP IS THE OCEAN

(How High Is the Sky)

ALTO SAX

Words and Music by
IRVING BERLIN

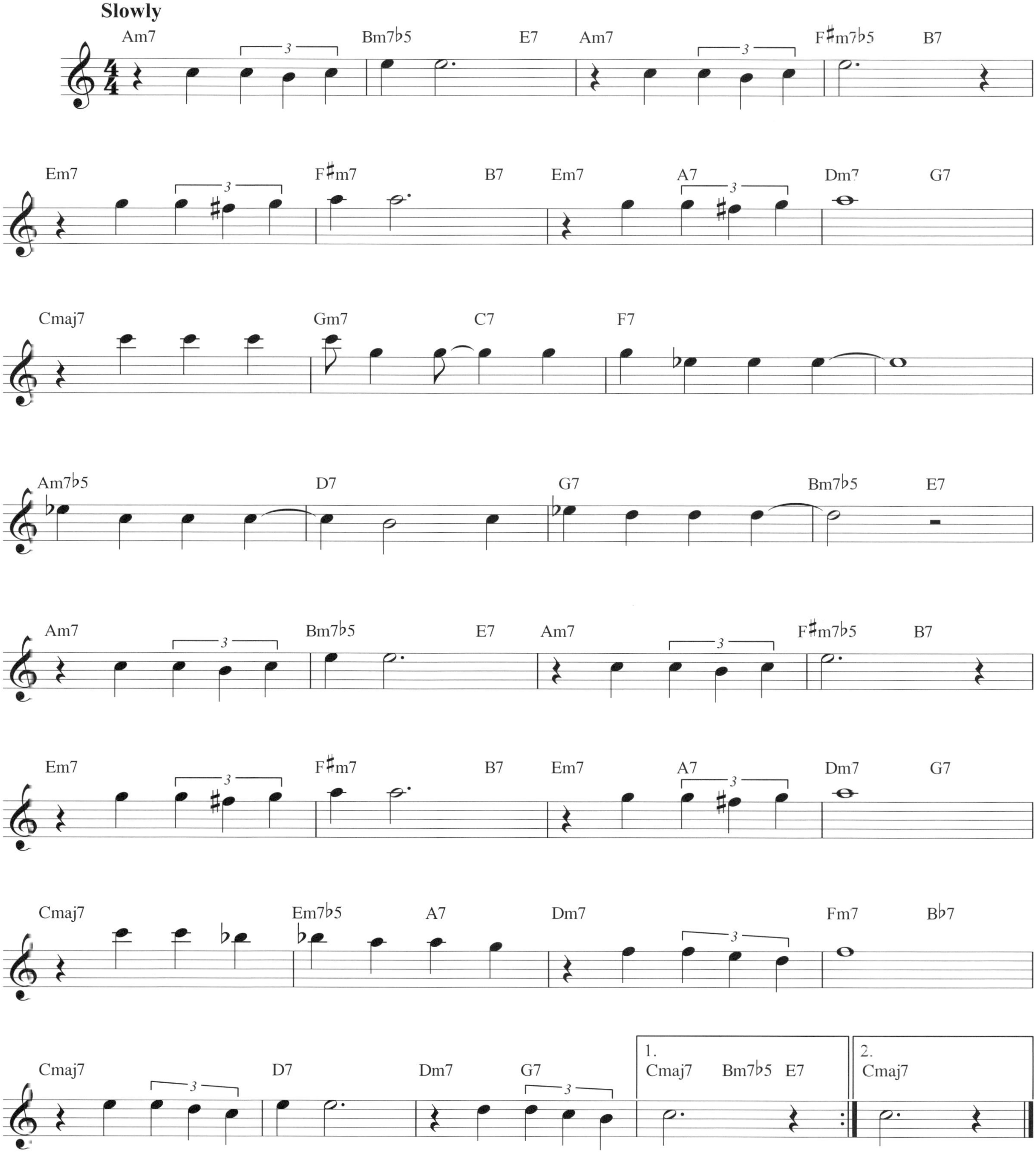

Slowly

Am7 Bm7♭5 E7 Am7 F♯m7♭5 B7

Em7 F♯m7 B7 Em7 A7 Dm7 G7

Cmaj7 Gm7 C7 F7

Am7♭5 D7 G7 Bm7♭5 E7

Am7 Bm7♭5 E7 Am7 F♯m7♭5 B7

Em7 F♯m7 B7 Em7 A7 Dm7 G7

Cmaj7 Em7♭5 A7 Dm7 Fm7 B♭7

Cmaj7 D7 Dm7 G7 1. Cmaj7 Bm7♭5 E7 2. Cmaj7

HOW INSENSITIVE

(Insensatez)

Music by ANTONIO CARLOS JOBIM
Original Words by VINICIUS DE MORAES
English Words by NORMAN GIMBEL

ALTO SAX

I CAN'T GET STARTED

ALTO SAX

Words by IRA GERSHWIN
Music by VERNON DUKE

I COULD WRITE A BOOK

ALTO SAX

Words by LORENZ HART
Music by RICHARD RODGERS

I GOT IT BAD AND THAT AIN'T GOOD

ALTO SAX

Words by PAUL FRANCIS WEBSTER
Music by DUKE ELLINGTON

I'LL REMEMBER APRIL

ALTO SAX

Words and Music by PAT JOHNSTON, DON RAYE AND GENE DE PAUL

Moderately

C C6 Cmaj7 C6 Cm7

Cm6 Cm7 Cm6 Dm7 G7

B♭9 A9 A7 Dm7 G7♭9 Cmaj7 C6

Fm7 B♭7 E♭maj7 E♭6 Fm7

B♭7 E♭maj7 E♭6 3 Dm7 G7

Cmaj7 C6 Bm7 E9 3 Amaj7 A6 Dm7 G7

C C6 Cmaj7 C6 Cm7

Cm6 Cm7 Cm6 Dm7 G7 3

B♭9 A9 A7 Dm7 G7♭9 C

I'M BEGINNING TO SEE THE LIGHT

ALTO SAX

Words and Music by DON GEORGE, JOHNNY HODGES, DUKE ELLINGTON and HARRY JAMES

I'VE GOT THE WORLD ON A STRING

ALTO SAX

Words by TED KOEHLER
Music by HAROLD ARLEN

IF I WERE A BELL

ALTO SAX

By FRANK LOESSER

IMAGINATION

ALTO SAX

Words by JOHNNY BURKE
Music by JIMMY VAN HEUSEN

Slowly, with a lilt

C C♯dim7 Dm7 G7 C Gm/B♭

A7 Dm7 A+ Dm7 G9 1. Em7 A7

Dm7 G7 2. C Gm7 C9 F

F♯m7 B7 Em7 A7 A♯dim7 G/B

Am7 D7 G G9 G7♯5 C C♯dim7

Dm7 G7 C Gm/B♭ A7 Dm7 A+

Dm7 G7 E7 A7 Dm7 Fm

Dm7 G7♭9 1. C C♯dim7 Dm7 G7 **D.S.** 2. C B♭ C

IN A SENTIMEMTAL MOOD

IN THE WEE SMALL HOURS OF THE MORNING

ALTO SAX

Words by BOB HILLIARD
Music by DAVID MANN

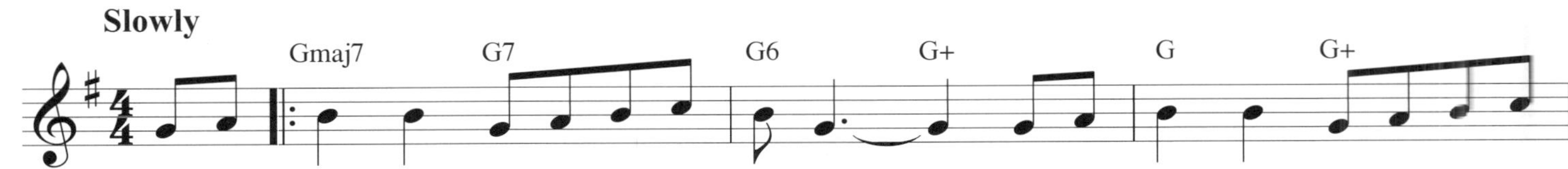

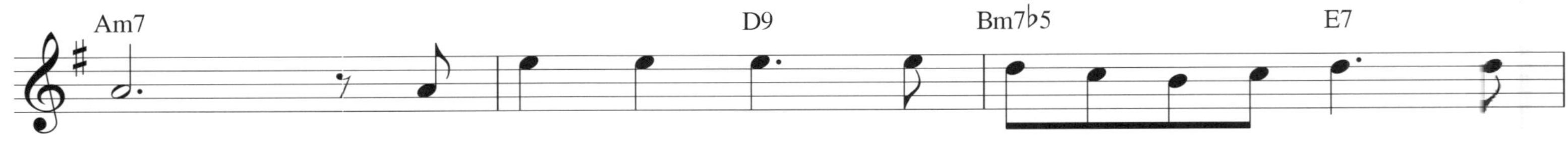

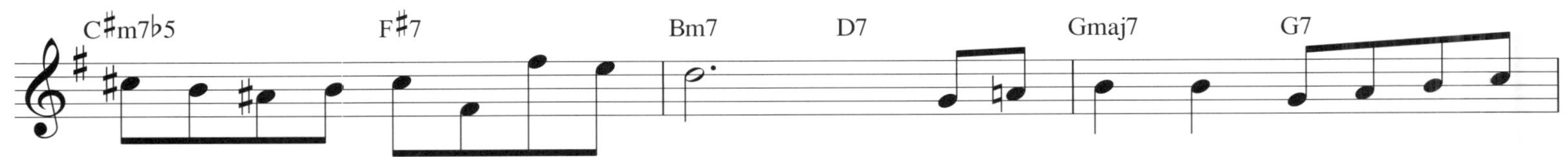

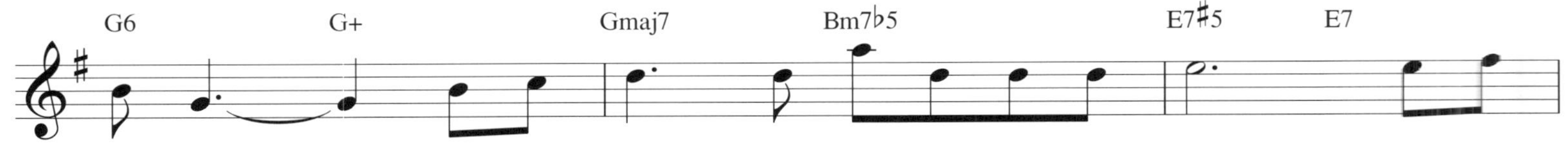

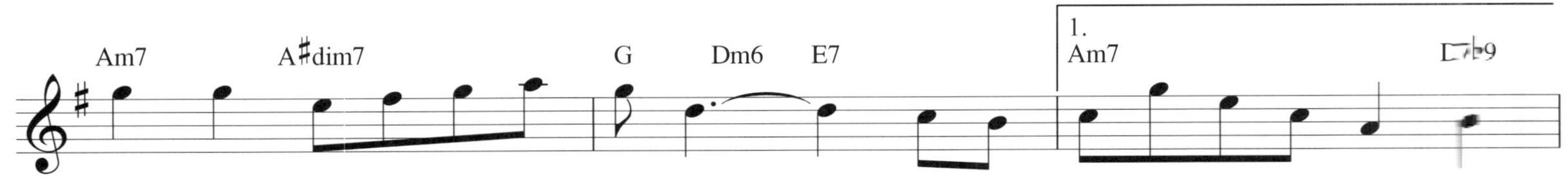

INDIANA

(Back Home Again in Indiana)

ALTO SAX

Words by BALLARD MacDONALD
Music by JAMES F. HANLEY

Moderately, with a lilt

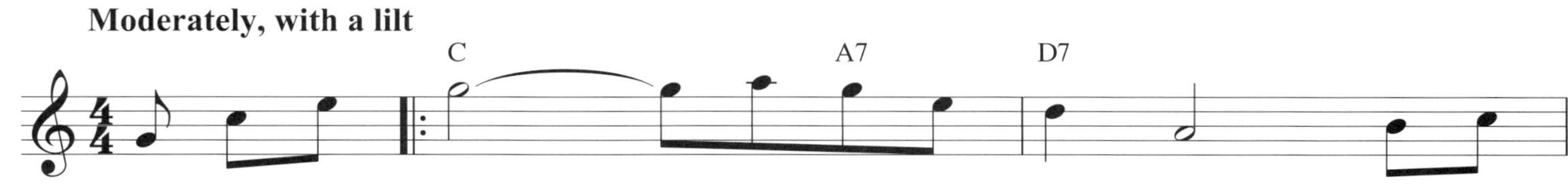

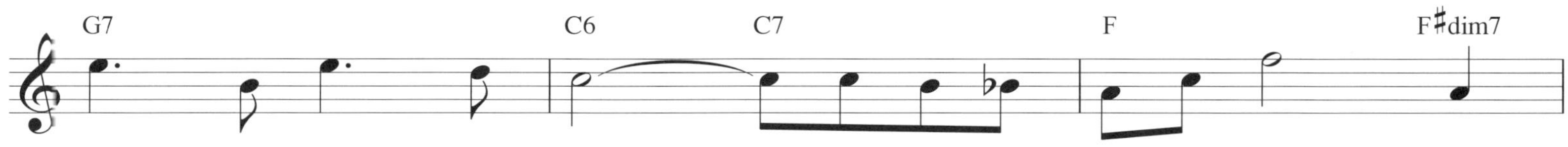

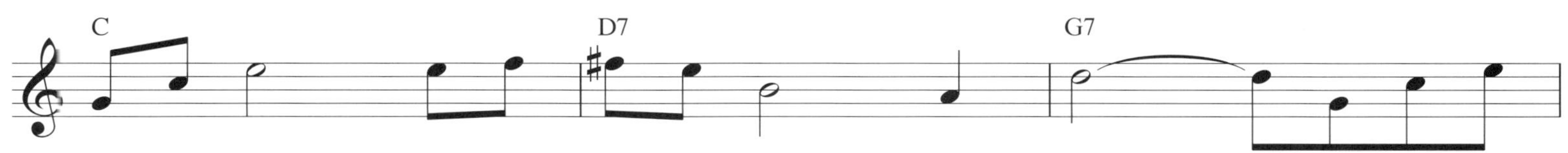

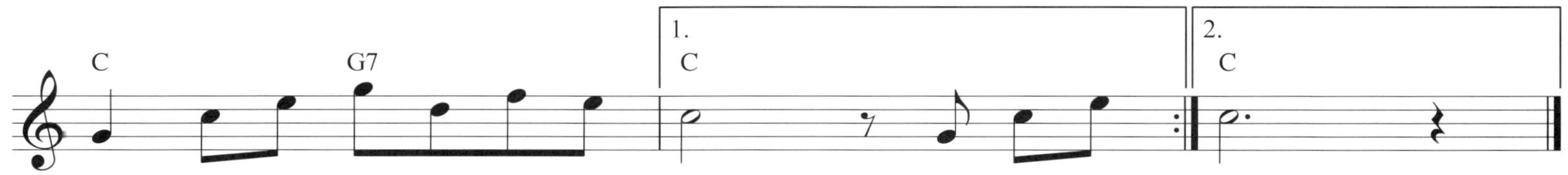

ISN'T IT ROMANTIC?

ALTO SAX

Words by LORENZ HART
Music by RICHARD RODGERS

Easy Swing

C G7 C G7♯5
C G7 C G7 C
A7♭9 Dm G7 E7 Am E7 Am C7
F A7 Dm G7 G♯dim7 Am D7 Gdim7 G7
C G7 C G7♯5 C G7 C
G7 C A7♭9 Dm G7 E7
Am Am7/G F♯m7♭5 Fm Em7 E♭7 Dm7 G7
1. C Am7 Dm7 G7 2. C

IT COULD HAPPEN TO YOU

ALTO SAX

Words by JOHNNY BURKE
Music by JAMES VAN HEUSEN

IT DON'T MEAN A THING
(If It Ain't Got That Swing)

ALTO SAX

Words and Music by DUKE ELLINGTON
and IRVING MILLS

IT MIGHT AS WELL BE SPRING

ALTO SAX

Lyrics by OSCAR HAMMERSTEIN II
Music by RICHARD RODGERS

THE LADY IS A TRAMP

LAZY RIVER

ALTO SAX

Words and Music by HOAGY CARMICHAEL
and SIDNEY ARODIN

Moderate Swing

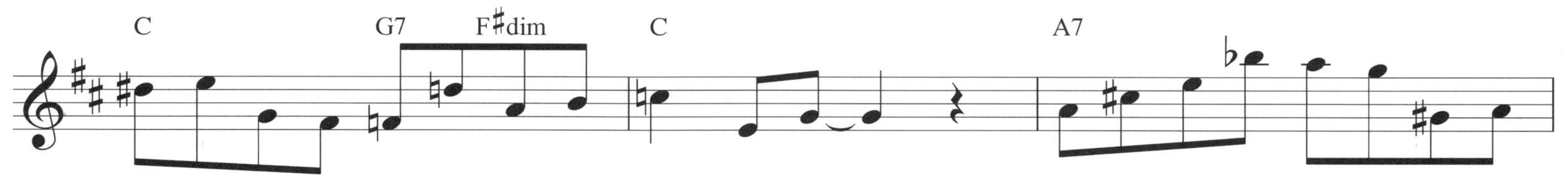

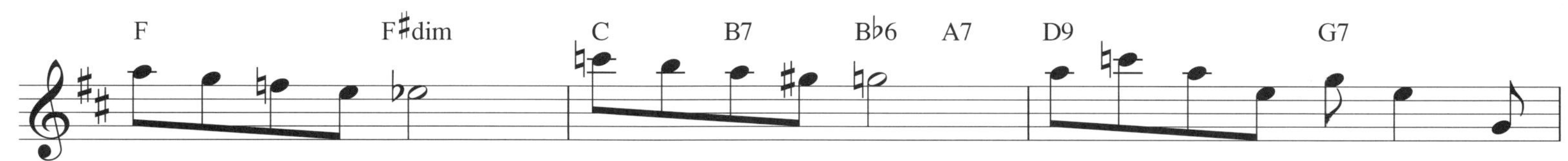

LET THERE BE LOVE

ALTO SAX

Lyric by IAN GRANT
Music by LIONEL RAND

LIKE SOMEONE IN LOVE

ALTO SAX

Words by JOHNNY BURKE
Music by JIMMY VAN HEUSEN

LITTLE GIRL BLUE

ALTO SAX

Words by LORENZ HART
Music by RICHARD RODGERS

LONG AGO (AND FAR AWAY)

ALTO SAX

Words by IRA GERSHWIN
Music by JEROME KERN

Moderately slow

D6 Bm7 Em7 A7 Dmaj7 Em7 A9

D6 Em7 A7 D6 C9 B7 Em7 A7

F6 Dm7 Gm7 C9 Fmaj7 E7

Amaj7 F♯m7 B7♭9 Em7 A7 D6 Bm7

Em7 A7 Dmaj7 Em7 A9 D6

Em7 A7 D6 C9 B7 Em7 A7 Am7

D7 Gmaj7 C9 D6/F♯ Fdim7

Em7 A7 1. D6 Bm7 Em7 A7 2. D6

LOVER, COME BACK TO ME

ALTO SAX

Lyrics by OSCAR HAMMERSTEIN II
Music by SIGMUND ROMBERG

LULLABY OF BIRDLAND

ALTO SAX

Words by GEORGE DAVID WEISS
Music by GEORGE SHEARING

Moderate Swing

Dm Bm7♭5 E7♭9 A7♭9 Dm7 Gm7 C9

Fmaj7 Dm7 Gm7 C7♭9 1. Fmaj7

Em7♭5 A7 2. Fmaj7 C7 Fmaj7 D9 D7♭9

Gm7 C9 C7♭9 Fmaj7 D9 D7♭9

Gm7 C9 C7♭9 Fmaj7 A7 Dm Bm7♭5

E7♭9 A7♭9 Dm7 Gm7 C9 Fmaj7 Dm7

Gm7 C7♭9 1. Fmaj7 Em7♭5 A7 **D.C.**

2. Fmaj7 Gm7 C9 Fmaj7 B♭9 Gm7 F♯9 F6/9

LULLABY OF THE LEAVES

ALTO SAX

Words by JOE YOUNG
Music by BERNICE PETKERE

Moderately

Am Emaj7 E7 A7 Dm7

Bm7 E7 Bm7 E7 1. Am F7 E7 2. Am Dm

Am Dm7

A Amaj7 A6 Dm7

A A#dim7 E7 Cdim E7

Am Emaj7 E7 A7 Dm7 Bm7 E7

Bm7 E7 1. Am Dm F7 E7 **D.C.** 2. Am Dm Am

MANHATTAN

ALTO SAX

Words by LORENZ HART
Music by RICHARD RODGERS

Medium Swing

C C/E E♭dim7 Dm G7 C

E♭dim7 Dm7 G7 Dm7 G7♯5 C Dm7 G7

C C/E E♭dim7 Dm G7 G♯dim7 Am Em E♭dim7

D7 Dm7 G7 Dm G7

C A7 Dm G7 C E♭dim7

Dm7 G7 Dm7 G7 Em7♭5 A7 Dm7

Fm C D7 C C/E E♭dim7

D7 G7 1. C Dm7 G7 2. C F C

MEDITATION

(Meditação)

ALTO SAX

Music by ANTONIO CARLOS JOBIM
Original Words by NEWTON MENDONÇA
English Words by NORMAN GIMBEL

MIDNIGHT SUN

ALTO SAX

Words and Music by LIONEL HAMPTON, SONNY BURKE and JOHNNY MERCER

MISTY

ALTO SAX
Music by ERROLL GARNER
Slowly, with a smooth Swing
Cmaj7 Gm7 C7♭9 Fmaj7
Fm B♭9 Cmaj7 Am Dm7 G7♭9
1. E7♭9 A7 D7♭5 G7 G9
2. C Am7 Dm7 G7♭9 C6
Gm7 C7♭9 Fmaj7 F6
F♯m7 B7 D7
G7 C♯dim7 Dm7 G7♭9 G9 Cmaj7 Gm7 C7♭9
Fmaj7 Fm B♭9 Cmaj7 Am
Dm7 G7♭9
1. C A7 D7♭5 G7 D.S.
2. C Fmaj7 Em7 C♯7 Cmaj7

MOOD INDIGO

ALTO SAX

Words and Music by DUKE ELLINGTON,
IRVING MILLS and ALBANY BIGARD

MOONLIGHT IN VERMONT

ALTO SAX

Words by JOHN BLACKBURN
Music by KARL SUESSDORF

Moderately

C6 Am7 Dm7 Db7#9 C6 Am7 Bb9

Dm7 G7sus C Dm7 G7 C6 Am7 Dm7 Db7#9

C6 Am7 Bb9 Dm7 G7sus C

F#m11 B7 Emaj7 E#dim7 F#m11 F9#11

Emaj7 E6 Gm11 C7 Fmaj7 F#dim7

Gm11 C9 F G7#5(b9) C6 Am7

Dm7 Db7#9 C6 Am7 Bb9 Dm7 G7sus

C Am7 D9 Db9 1. Cmaj9 Dm7 G7 2. Cmaj9

MORE THAN YOU KNOW

ALTO SAX

Words by WILLIAM ROSE and EDWARD ELISCU
Music by VINCENT YOUMANS

MY HEART STOOD STILL

ALTO SAX

Words by LORENZ HART
Music by RICHARD RODGERS

Moderately

D Fdim7 Em7 A7 D D+ Em7 A7

D D+ G6 A9 D Em7 A7 D Fdim7

Em7 A7 D D+ Em7 A7 D D+

G6 A9 D G6 D Dm6

A+ A Bm7♭5 E7

A7♯5 A7 D Fdim7

Em7 A7 D F♯+ G Em7

D/A A7 1. D Em7 A7 2. D

MY OLD FLAME

ALTO SAX

Words and Music by ARTHUR JOHNSTON
and SAM COSLOW

Moderate Swing

Dmaj7 F♯dim7 B7♭9 Em7 Gm7 A7

Dmaj7 Gm7 C7 Fmaj7 B♭7 Em7 A7 Dmaj7

F♯m7♭5 B7♭9 Em7 Gm7 A7 Dmaj7 Gm7 C7

Fmaj7 B♭7 Em7 A7 Dmaj7 Gm7 C7 Fmaj7

Gm7 C7 E♭7 D7 G7 Gm7 C7

Em7♭5 A7 Dm7 Bm7 E7 Em7 A7 Dmaj7

F♯m7♭5 B7♭9 Em7 Gm7 A7 Dmaj7 Gm7 C7

Fmaj7 B♭7 Em7 A7♯5 1. Dmaj7 Em7 A7 2. Dmaj7

MY ONE AND ONLY LOVE

MY ROMANCE

ALTO SAX

Words by LORENZ HART
Music by RICHARD RODGERS

MY SHIP

ALTO SAX

Words by IRA GERSHWIN
Music by KURT WEILL

THE NEARNESS OF YOU

A NIGHT IN TUNISIA

ALTO SAX

By JOHN "DIZZY" GILLESPIE
and FRANK PAPARELLI

Moderately fast Swing

C7 Bm C7 Bm

C7 Bm C♯m7♭5 F♯7♭5 1. Bm 2. Bm **Fine**

F♯m7♭5 B7♭9 Em6 B7♭9 Em6

Em7♭5 A7♭9 D6 C♯m7♭5 F♯7♭5 C7

Bm C7 Bm C7 Bm

C♯m7♭5 F♯7♭5 Bm C♯m7♭5

C7♯11 Bm

E7♯11 Em(maj7) Em7

D♯7♯9 Dmaj7 C♯m7♭5 F♯7♭9 **D.S. al Fine (take repeat)**

ON GREEN DOLPHIN STREET

ALTO SAX

Lyrics by NED WASHINGTON
Music by BRONISLAU KAPER

ONE NOTE SAMBA

(Samba de uma nota so)

ALTO SAX

Original Lyrics by NEWTON MENDONÇA
English Lyrics by ANTONIO CARLOS JOBIM
Music by ANTONIO CARLOS JOBIM

PICK YOURSELF UP

ALTO SAX

Words by DOROTHY FIELDS
Music by JEROME KERN

Moderately fast Swing

Dm7 G7 Cmaj7 Fmaj7 Bm7♭5 E7♭9 Am7 D7

G7sus G7 Em7 A7 Dm7 G7 C Em7 A7

Dmaj7 Gmaj7 C♯m7♭5 F♯7♭9 Bm7 E7 A7sus A7 F♯m7 B7

Em7 A7 D E♭maj7 E♭6 E♭maj7 E♭6

E♭7 B♭7 E♭ E♭6 E♭7 G

Em7 A9 Dm7 G7 Dm7 G7 Cmaj7 Fmaj7 Bm7♭5 E7♭9

Am7 D7 Gmaj7 G7 G6 G+ Em Em7/D C♯m7♭5

Dm7 G7sus G7 1. C G7 2. C

POLKA DOTS AND MOONBEAMS

ALTO SAX

Words by JOHNNY BURKE
Music by JIMMY VAN HEUSEN

QUIET NIGHTS OF QUIET STARS
(Corcovado)

ALTO SAX

English Words by GENE LEES
Original Words and Music by ANTONIO CARLOS JOBIM

SATIN DOLL

ALTO SAX

By DUKE ELLINGTON

SKYLARK

ALTO SAX

Words by JOHNNY MERCER
Music by HOAGY CARMICHAEL

SO NICE
(Summer Samba)

ALTO SAX

Original Words and Music by MARCOS VALLE
and PAULO SERGIO VALLE
English Words by NORMAN GIMBEL

SOPHISTICATED LADY

ALTO SAX

Words and Music by DUKE ELLINGTON,
IRVING MILLS and MITCHELL PARISH

SPEAK LOW

ALTO SAX

Words by OGDEN NASH
Music by KURT WEILL

STELLA BY STARLIGHT

ALTO SAX

Words by NED WASHINGTON
Music by VICTOR YOUNG

STOMPIN' AT THE SAVOY

ALTO SAX

By BENNY GOODMAN,
EDGAR SAMPSON and CHICK WEBB

STORMY WEATHER

(Keeps Rainin' All the Time)

ALTO SAX

Lyric by TED KOEHLER
Music by HAROLD ARLEN

A SUNDAY KIND OF LOVE

ALTO SAX

Words and Music by LOUIS PRIMA, ANITA NYE LEONARD, STANLEY RHODES and BARBARA BELLE

TANGERINE

ALTO SAX
Words by JOHNNY MERCER
Music by VICTOR SCHERTZINGER
Easy Swing
Em7 A7 D
D/F♯ Fdim7 Em7 A7 Em7 A7 Dmaj7
B7♭9 B7♯5 Em7 A7 D C♯7
F♯ D♯m7 G♯m7 C♯9 F♯7 B9 B7♯5
Em7 A7 D D/F♯ Fdim7 Em7 A7
Em7 A7 F♯7 F♯7♭5 B9 Em Em/D 3
C♯m7 F♯7 Bm7 3 E7 Em7
A7♭9 1. D B7♭9 B7♯5 2. D

THERE'S A SMALL HOTEL

ALTO SAX

Words by LORENZ HART
Music by RICHARD RODGERS

THESE FOOLISH THINGS (REMIND ME OF YOU)

ALTO SAX

Words by HOLT MARVELL
Music by JACK STRACHEY

THE THINGS WE DID LAST SUMMER

THIS CAN'T BE LOVE

ALTO SAX

Words by LORENZ HART
Music by RICHARD RODGERS

THOU SWELL

ALTO SAX

Words by LORENZ HART
Music by RICHARD RODGERS

UNFORGETTABLE

ALTO SAX

Words and Music by
IRVING GORDON

Easy Swing

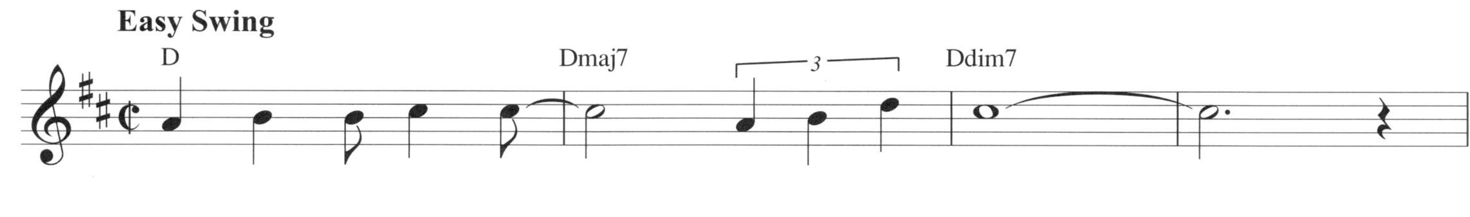

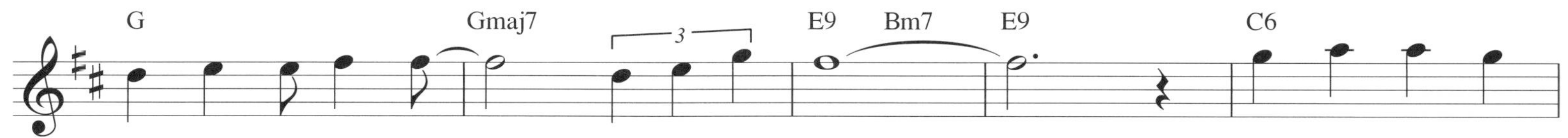

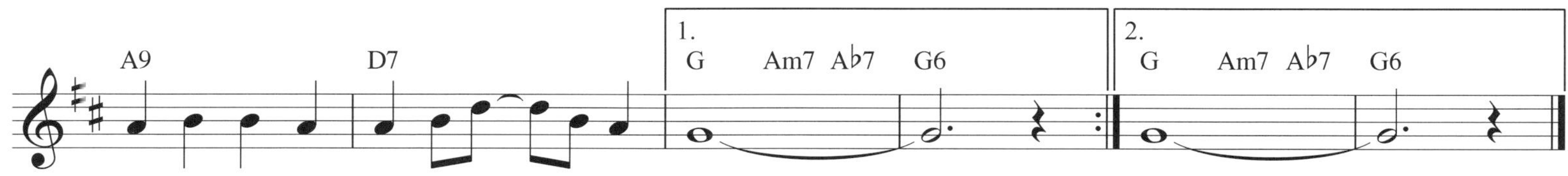

THE VERY THOUGHT OF YOU

ALTO SAX

Words and Music by
RAY NOBLE

WATCH WHAT HAPPENS

Music by MICHEL LEGRAND
Original French Text by JACQUES DEMY
English Lyrics by NORMAN GIMBEL

ALTO SAX

WAVE

ALTO SAX

Words and Music by
ANTONIO CARLOS JOBIM

THE WAY YOU LOOK TONIGHT

ALTO SAX

Words by DOROTHY FIELDS
Music by JEROME KERN

WHAT'LL I DO

ALTO SAX

Words and Music by
IRVING BERLIN

WILLOW WEEP FOR ME

WITCHCRAFT

ALTO SAX

Music by CY COLEMAN
Lyrics by CAROLYN LEIGH

YESTERDAYS

ALTO SAX

Words by OTTO HARBACH
Music by JEROME KERN

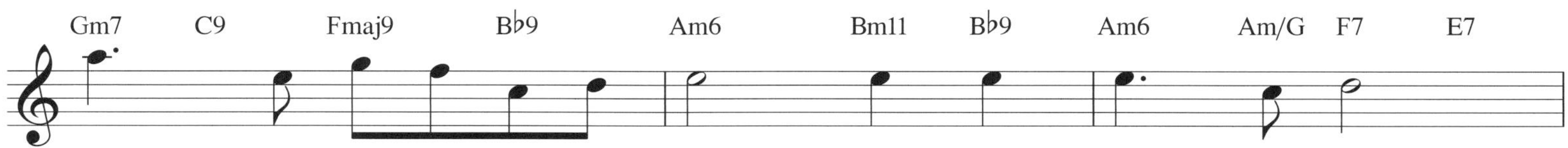

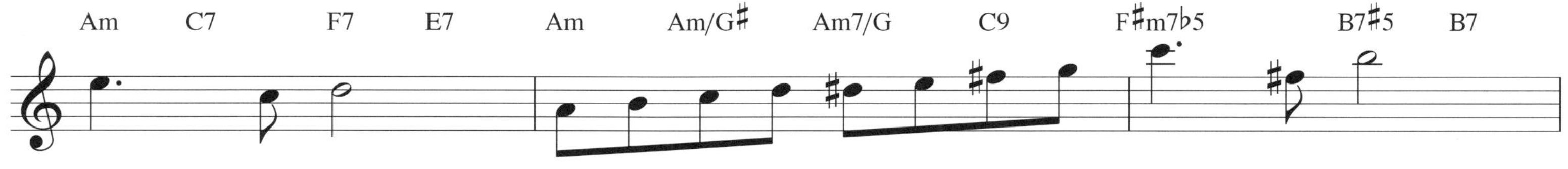

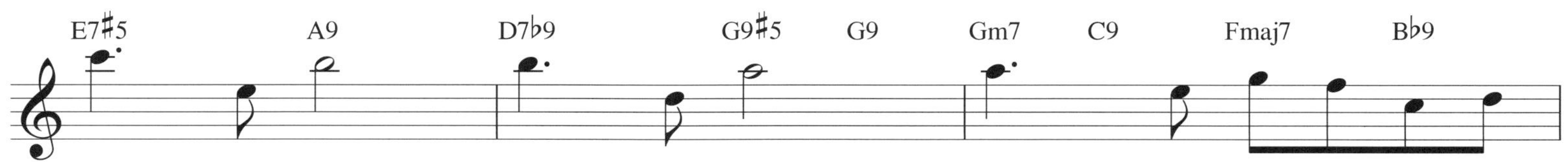

YOU ARE TOO BEAUTIFUL

ALTO SAX

Words by LORENZ HART
Music by RICHARD RODGERS

YOU BROUGHT A NEW KIND OF LOVE TO ME

YOU DON'T KNOW WHAT LOVE IS

ALTO SAX

Words and Music by DON RAYE
and GENE DePAUL